Let Me Testify

Let Me Testify

MESSAGES OF TRIUMPH, PURPOSE AND SURVIVAL

AN ANTHOLOGY FROM

SURVIVAL RADIO CHRISTIAN NETWORK

Copyright © 2013 Survival Radio Christian Network

Expected End Entertainment

All rights reserved.

ISBN-10:0988554518

ISBN-13: 978-0-9885545-1-1

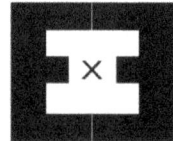

Dedication

Let Me Testify: Messages of Triumph, Purpose and Survival is dedicated to all of the listeners and supporters of The Survival Radio Christian Network, its shows, and its hosts. Thank you for your continued support as we strive to a blessing to the world.

Table of Contents

INTRODUCTION..1
C. NATHANIEL BROWN

REJECTION..3
CLARENCE WHITE III

DESIRE A PURPOSE DRIVEN RELATIONSHIP.................23
OMON KENNETH ONI-ESELEH, PH.D

THE LIGHT...35
J.B. MCGEE

TRANSFORMATION..49
JOHNNETTE YOUNG

LOVE DOESN'T HURT..59
JOYCE WHITE

I WAS BORN FOR THIS...73
JOY MARINO

MASTER CAN YOU USE ME...................................79
LARRY MCKENZIE

SMELL THE ROSE...83
SHARON D. GREEN

DELIVERED FOR HIS USE.....................................103
TANYA LEWIS

BECOMING WHO I WAS BORN TO BE......................113
TERRELLE LEWIS

BORN INTO ROYALTY..123
YOLANDA POWELL

Let Me Testify

INTRODUCTION

There comes a time in everyone's life when they realize the world does not revolve around them. And for Christians that epiphany extends beyond the surface. We are charged with becoming disciples of Jesus Christ and sharing out faith, our beliefs, and our experiences of being children of God. We are to go into all of the world, proclaiming the Gospel of our Lord and Savior Jesus Christ, and having an impact on a lost and dying world.

How do we do that? The Bible says in Revelation 12:11 that, *"They triumphed over him by the blood of the Lamb and by the word of their testimony; and they did not love their lives so much as to shrink from death."*

Let Me Testify: Messages of Triumph, Purpose and Survival is the culmination of like-spirited, like-minded individuals bringing their testimonies, stories, experiences, and perspectives into one book to fulfill the Great Commission and have an impact on our surroundings. The Survival Radio Christian Network is one of the fastest growing networks on the airwaves with some of the most anointed hosts that include ministers, entrepreneurs, speakers, teachers, and much more. Our mission is to provide spiritually uplifting and encouraging radio programming that magnifies Jesus Christ, edifies other Christians, and introduce newcomers to the Kingdom of God.

Let Me Testify is our first project as a network outside of the individual shows. The hosts have shared transparent testimonies of their deliverance, how they discovered their callings, and how we ought to live in victory as Christians, just to name a few topics.

We strongly believe that you will be blessed by this book and other projects coming from the Survival Radio Christian Network in the near future. We are committed to bringing our listeners and our supporters the best programming and products that will represent who we are as Christians. We welcome your feedback, your comments, and your continued support. So please visit our website at **www.survivalradiochristiannetwork.com** and share with us.

Thank you in advance for supporting The Survival Radio Christian Network. Our prayer is that you are blessed by Let Me Testify: Messages of Triumph, Purpose and Survival.

C. Nathaniel Brown
President

Rejection

BY CLARENCE WHITE III

REJECTION was the first word that I heard the prayer minister say. I am still not certain why I responded to the call for prayer that Sunday morning at The Kingdom Builders Center, but something in me was compelled to go. There was nothing specifically wrong in my life and I had no specific prayer request when I mirrored the posture of prayer of everyone else in line. There was nothing specific as everything seemed to be going wrong in my life.

My spouse and I were at constant odds. Mostly over financial strains as she had been the consequence of an organizational downsize, and my salary was insufficient to cover all of our needs. Our blended family, including his and her children, and the assortment of other parents was also a source of perpetual stress. The children that I gained through marriage, my wife's teenage daughters from her first marriage, could not have been more obstinate at this point. My relationship with them had deteriorated to one of silence. They did not speak to me and I did not speak to them. We were all being childish. My children, who are from three different relationships and live in three different places, seemed to be affected by whatever particles of weirdness that was falling from the sky.

My oldest son was having difficulty adjusting to sixth grade; choosing a reputation of coolness over academic excellence that he had earned up to this point. So far, my methods of encouraging him to excellence had weak results against the four states distance that stands between us. My youngest son celebrated a gold medal in the nine and ten year old division of his first statewide Kuk Sol Woon martial arts tournament, and then, coincidentally, he managed to get into a physical altercation every week for the next three weeks. Finally, my oldest child, my only daughter, who I adopted nearly nine years ago when she was 13, was still reeling from a break-up that occurred more than a year ago. For the record, it hurts when the pain you have caused others visits upon your children. I mean I was only slightly guilty of the offenses of all my children, and now it seems that karma has arrived.

Considering the state of my marriage, troubles with our children, lack of security in my career, concerns over my health, recent dejection in ministry and sadness over the progressing dementia of our last remaining grandparent, how could I possibly have one prayer request? It was not possible. So, I did not present any concerns. I only took a posture of prayer and displayed a willingness to receive any word from God. So I approached the designated spot for prayer, bowed my head and stretched out my arms with my palms facing upward, and I waited patiently for a word.

I was completely prepared for the Holy Ghost to take over the prayer. The list in my mind was long and I figured that any improvement would be a blessing. Hearing the word REJECTION, however, was unexpected. This word opened a reservoir of emotions that had long been forgotten. The fear and pain of rejection was obviously still present in my life, yet I did not recognize this to be the case. Admittedly, I immediately begin to search for a parallel between my current issues and the feelings of rejection that were surfacing. This reflection, my current testimony involves how I came to terms with feelings of rejection, and how the victory will benefit me and my loved ones.

I had questions, but it was not appropriate to ask them during the prayer. And I was too emotional afterwards to dare open my mouth – tears would have certainly replaced any words. First of all, how could I have been dealing with rejection? I am strong, brave, courageous, a fighter, a conqueror, a lover, full of forgiveness, a minister of Jesus Christ, which means I fully embrace redemption, and I promote releasing self and others to their best life possible despite our past. The way that I saw myself is how I hoped others received me. Why did the Holy Ghost reveal this word to the prayer minister? And why reveal this now? In the end, hearing that word helped me to realize exactly what I was running from – a fear of rejection.

My fear of rejection did not start with my marriage. Our children are certainly not a threat to my fears. Seldom have I relied completely on any career, so economic displacement holds little on my peace. I have been without as much as a place to sleep – completely in transition from one sofa to another floor space for weeks. Therefore, the real source of my fear of rejection must have been buried far deeper than my present concerns.

I began the healing process by looking back over the course of my life starting as far back as I could remember. I wondered how many different ways I had allowed rejection to manifest in my life – through fear, doubt, criticism, cynicism, anger, depression, hopelessness, recklessness, and withdrawal. The latter was the sting after the bite. For weeks prior to this revelatory prayer I had been asking God why did I withdraw so easily from past relationships? Family, friends, fraternity, classmates, coworkers, acquaintances, flings, or whatever the nature of the relationship - I have mastered the art of walking away.

My mental journey took me to my beginning. I began this reflection with the events surrounding my birth. Obviously, I have no personal recollection of these events. My memory is only of accounts provided by each of my parents and my grandparent that was involved. I was given to my maternal grandmother at birth and remained with her for three years. For three years Momma, my maternal grandmother held exclusive custody of me.

Here is what I know. My mother discovered she was pregnant midway in her sophomore year of college at the Florida A&M University. My father was not a student, but rather a local. He still is tall, handsome, well-dress, smooth-talking, and known for always having the latest car. Reportedly, he was a real catch for any woman. My mother is extraordinarily bright as exhibited by her earned doctorate of philosophy. Her academic excellence is matched with a beautiful face and great personal style, which her high school year book confirms through senior accolades. My mother has always been a social queen, and her popularity and other features obviously drew the attention of my father. Their attraction led to a pregnancy.

The pregnancy resulted in a lifestyle change for both of my parents. My father gained a military career and my mother accepted a full-time job as a telephone operator. And I landed with my grandmother. My grandmother worked also, but she accepted the opportunity to care for her first grandchild.

According to both my parents, the arrangement was meant to be temporary, but either the routine grew comfortable or no one wanted to break the bond I had with my grandmother. There is no telling how long I would have stayed if I had not referred to my father as 'that damn Clarence' one random afternoon. I was promptly removed from my grandmother's care.

Countless stories of my first three years draw a conclusion about who we were as individuals and a family. These stories explain what I did, who I was, and with whom; yet, they never seemed to adequately resolve the lingering question of why. Certainly my father who served in the United States Army during Vietnam did not benefit the most, or my mother who worked in the evenings as a telephone operator and attended college full-time, or my grandmother who also worked full-time and cared for me. It must have been me that received the greatest benefit from the arrangement.

I think of each of their sacrifices now that I have a family to care for. There are times when I want to be selfish. Yet, as the example was set for me I place the things I desire on a shelf for the best interest of my wife and children. I am grateful for the early and often examples of each of my caretakers. But, am I wrong for considering their motivations, especially as I look for answers to my current dilemma?

It stands to reason that I would question motives. Was I not desired, since I was not planned? Did my parents hold resentment towards each other, and me for the marriage that resulted from my birth? And, if the pregnancy did not cause resentment during a time when out of wedlock pregnancies were a huge stigma, then certainly having to attend school, work full time or enlist in the military could cause resent? I mean – my mother delayed academic opportunities and forfeited social influence in order to give me life. And I had the audacity to be a sickly child with bronchitis and a number of other ailments. Thank God abortions were not considered a form of birth control when I was conceived.

Let's be clear. I am certainly not the first child to be reared by a grandparent for any length of time. Nor am I complaining that it was a terrible idea or horrible act of injustice. However, I wonder if even then as an infant, in some conscious state if I knew rejection, abandonment, or the nature of being a burden. Of course not! Everything that surrounds my early years proves that I knew love, affection, care, and nurturing.

What about subconsciously? Could I have felt a sense of displacement because I was not with my mother and father? How could I have possibly known the differences between the love that I had received and the love that God designed for me to have? Were the two loves the same? In the end, I resolved that any impact from these earlier years, if any, were nominal. My concerns of rejection could not be buried that deep in subconscious during my first three years.

These unanswered questions, however, made me that much more intentional about breaking the silence between my children. I want them to have access to me now, so that they will have few unresolved inquiries later in life. I am more resolute because of this journey to endure their growing pains and to be more compassionate and less demanding that they adhere to my system of rearing.

As I continued to search for answers to the original question of rejection many stories, detailed and ambiguous incidents, and meaningful faces appeared. The time span ranged from just a few weeks ago to the time when I was four or five and playing with cousins. I remembered interactions with family members, neighbors who were just like family, school mates, business partners, fraternity brothers, and of course, lovers. An interesting sub-pattern began to form of attachment, disappointment, and ultimately withdrawal.

My journey was taking a new direction. I wanted more than ever to reach out to folks from my past and plead for their forgiveness. I wanted to share with them that my collection of unresolved hurt led to me hurting them. Yet, I also realized that my desire to seek these persons' forgiveness was selfish. These folks could be living prefect lives without me. What about the further harm I could cause by digging up their unresolved pain - pain that I caused? If they ever need me then I hope they find me and we take that journey together.

After resolving to stick to the current issue of rejection I returned to my chronological expedition. I reunited with my parents at the age of three and within two years they were divorced. It continues to strike me as odd that I have no feelings towards their divorce. I remember the excitement that I had for the Christmas before the divorce. The picturesque morning with a small living room filled with presents still ranks as my most favored Christmas morning. I remember the concern over learning that my mother was in the hospital later that year from a bad fall down a flight of concrete stairs. Certainly the fall was the consequence of platform heels. I remember grief from the passing of my great-grandmother on my sixth birthday as she dressed for my party. Yet, I have no recollection of feeling anything about the divorce.

In part, I wonder if my lack of emotion is due to the absence of change. My father is an active figure in my life. He was an even bigger part of my life immediately after the divorce. I remember attending church with him, especially the stops on the way to church for Lifesavers candy as a bride to remain quiet during worship. I recall travelling with my father and spending time with him at various family members' homes. I cannot recall any impact or significant change that the divorce had on my relationship with either parent.

In addition, these were the days when communities were really tight knit, and any child was everyone's child. So, I have memories of a lot of people that felt like family because they helped my mother care for me and my sister. Primarily, the family interactions that I remember most vividly during those years is with my grandmother, my god-family, and a certain set of cousins.

My Big Daddy, sort of like a god-grandfather, and his family was the single most uplifting group of people that were not related by blood that have ever loved me. In the eyes of my god-family I could do no wrong – I was perfect. In my eyes, as long as they were watching over me, then nothing seemed impossible. Has there ever been anyone in your life that inspired confidence? I was fearless with them, and I can imagine fearful to others because of the confidence they inspired in me. Big Daddy was a hero and I would do anything to make him laugh and hear how proud he was of his Popcorn, me. His wife, sons, and daughters brought equal joy and confidence, and in return I delivered them the best of my tales from the playgrounds and school. They were as much a permanent attachment as my parents.

Through my own divorce I learned unintentional consequences. Often our decisions affect the innocence of others that we have no intentions of causing harm. I now have a son that is separated from a community of people, including family members that want to know and love him. Certainly my parents did not intend for the relationships that I developed with my grandmother, Big Daddy or cousins to be affected by their decisions. Reflecting on this part of my story, and my own divorce helps me to realize that every incision causes pain, even if it ultimately leads to some form of good.

These experiences that happened before I turned six years resonate with me as if they just happened. And there are many other stories and people that could be mentioned. My memories of these times hold no tears – only joy. I appreciate having a grandmother that loved her daughter enough to care for me. I am certain that my life would have been quite different without our Momma. The same can be said for my parents who I know made their decisions out of love for me. I was blessed with an extended family that was very intentional about assuring that I had the best childhood possible, even if it was not a textbook environment. We knew disdain, divorce, disappointment, and degradation. But, I also knew affirmation, attachment, and accomplishment. So, it is not possible that I knew rejection at this age.

As I continued the journey to discover the source of this fear of rejection it seemed logical to remain in those early years. However, my mind began to leap randomly through different periods of my life where I felt rejection. There was the first time that I wrote to pledge my fraternity and I did not receive a call. There was my senior year in high school when I lost the vote for Homecoming king. And I remember being overlooked for All Star honors in eighth grade, even though I felt I was one of the better defensive players on the team. There were so many random accounts of this negative feeling that spread across my life. Not surprisingly some of these accounts of rejection involved young girls from my adolescence and women throughout young adulthood. Thankfully I did not let rejection stand in the way of me pursuing purpose, intimacy, relationships, and love.

I believe in balance, and in this particular place in my life I look for the positive each aspect of my life. For every encounter with the feeling of rejection - I can remember a moment when I was affirmed. And when affirmation was not granted willingly by others, I know that God placed certain people in my life, such as Big Daddy that inspired confidence to keep on going. A great example of this is the founding of the Kings of Romance. I must share this part of my journey.

My high school had a pecking order. The order went something like this for guys. At the top of the list were the athletes, primarily football players, then basketball players. Other types of athletes received praise based on their starting positions or having their contributions recognized by a local or region publication. After the athletes, rankings were loosely based on neighborhood affiliations.

My time in high school predated gangs in Central Florida, so people tended to bond around either sports or neighborhoods. If you did not play an organized sport, but had credibility in your neighborhood, and your neighborhood was revered, then that level of respect transfer to school. Rankings also included certain band members; guys with money, which there were less than a handful in Gainesville,

Florida; and the guys that everyone knew could fight. Plenty of guys claimed to have good hands, but there were only a few that everyone knew not to mess with.

Frankly, in high school I did not fit in any one particular group. However, I was handsome, tall, smart, and dated some of the most sought after girls. Therefore, I was allowed to hang on the peripheral of these groups, but I was never given membership. The only natural thing for me to do was create my own category. Thus, the Kings of Romance were born.

Not to be denied my full rights of acceptance, I approached several of my classmates that were seniors and juniors that I shared the same problem I had. There is strength in numbers. I was the founder and president, and I recruited a local DJ, a quiet yet tough type that reminded me of the great Joe Louis, and the new kid at school. The new kid was a solid all around athlete, and he was '80's cute, meaning he had light skin, a Jeri curl, and bowed legs.
The ladies loved him. There were about six of us in all and we became the new Kings of the campus.

KOR went on to gain major respect throughout the remainder of my senior year. We held our own in every aspect, and we lavished in every moment. They say imitation is the highest form of flattery. Well a testament to our success included the other clubs that were founded that same year. The highest compliment in my opinion is that years later when I would visit the campus for nostalgia reasons I found that KOR lived on.

I received other positive affirmations throughout life. A sample of these encouraging moments looked like a teacher who recognized my academic success and asked me to take her advanced class. Or, a teacher who wanted to expand the breath of my experiences and invited me to be a leader in her church's youth ministry. And there was the teacher who was willing to develop my athleticism, because they recognized an ability to learn new things quickly. There was even a neighbor that provided the tools I needed to get my second business started when I was 10. I received affirmation from neighbors, church members, teachers, and fellow students. I can say with sincerity that there has always been at least one person that seemed to stand above any negativity and sow positivity into my life.

As I continued to reflect, it seemed that whatever feelings I hold towards rejection were already present during this period. The source could not have come from high school or college. I was pleased to remember as many positive interactions as I did challenging ones. In fact, the same could be said for the early years. So where did my issue reside? Certainly I had met rejection, but nothing so severe that I would have a life long battle.

I would argue that an acknowledgment of these feelings is a sign of health and balance. But, I would not rush to deny my concerns. Denial is just as big a problem in the mental health arena as is over exaggeration. Yet, through embracing this issue I begin to feel empowered by the possibility that this journey would make me a better husband, father, friend, and minister.

So, the mental expedition continued and I returned to the age of five where I begin to pick apart other fragmented experiences. A chain of events stood out for quite possibly the first time. Within the span of a year the divisions in my family became concrete. My father remarried, first, to the lady that would give birth to my little brother. Afterwards, my grandmother would get married, after being divorced for over 20 years. And finally, my mother fell in love and moved to Gainesville, Florida, a different part of the state – leaving me, and my younger sister this time with our grandmother and her new husband.

Obviously I was much more available for each of these unions, in regards to having an understanding of their significance to my life. My father's union had the least amount of impact because nothing changed in our routine. Our mother's move initially seemed reasonable. It was the summer time and we generally spent the bulk of summers with our grandmother anyway. It was explained and accepted that as soon as she got established that my sister and I would join her.

Our grandmother's marriage was not as easy to digest. The surroundings, the food, and the people all changed. We were not harmed – trust me we were not harmed because grandmother would have none of that, but the difference was notable. It never felt right and even now I still cannot articulate why.

The key event that I would describe as the first time I was aware of my feelings involved our grandmother, my sister, and our mother. It was the end of the summer and we were returning from a visit with family outside of Panama City, Florida. The drive is a little more than an hour back to Tallahassee. That weekend it seemed like forever since we had seen our mother, even though it was probably more like a few weeks. My sister and I fully expected to return with our mother to Gainesville where she had relocated with our soon to be new father. But on that trip back we were lured into a decision to stay with our grandmother for a little while longer. We were both heartbroken. This is my first memory of a heartbreak.

I am sure that it broke my heart when I was taken from my grandmother at three years old, but I do not remember that feeling. My parents' divorce must had been impactful, but with all of the love I received from each of my parents, and everything else that happened that year, I cannot say that I even noticed the event. But at the age of six, my heart was breaking.

My sister responded with tears. She is still the more emotionally transparent sibling. You will know exactly how she feels on everything. In more ways than one she has been the more mature sibling, even though I am three years older. Her maturity is why I have often included her in the list of the most influential people in my life.

I responded with silence and held in my emotions as I still do in most cases. The hard part was having the idea presented as a choice; we could stay with our grandmother, Momma, if we wanted to. Yet, I knew the decision was already made for us. We would begin the school year with our grandmother. In the end the time passed quick enough and our mother returned to get us in just a couple of months. We were in Gainesville before the turn of seasons, and to witness our mother marry the man who would rear us into adulthood.

The decision to leave us with our grandmother while our mother established a home for us just does seem significant enough to result in my concern over rejection. And, why would I have felt rejection at a tender age of six? Was there a lingering memory from my early childhood at that time? Did I yearn that much for affirmation from my mother? Was there a sense that I was not good enough for her, her first born and only son? I wondered if the status of favorite child by my great-grandmother and grandmother could have riled up some hidden emotion in my mother towards her own parent. Frankly, what could I feel like I was in competition for, or with whom? I have no answers for these and many more inquiries of myself, then or now.

Someone reading this may wonder why I have not asked

these questions, then, or now. My family is old fashion. Children are to be seen and not heard. We did as we were told, immediately after we were told to do it. Asking questions, even for clarification sake was not received well. So, we developed ingenuity at a very early age. We were intuitive and industrious because that is what it took to succeed. Success in all areas of our lives was important, especially in academics. Therefore, we leveraged our academic successes for the things we wanted or against our offenses. But we knew that a child stayed in a child's place. I could have never asked these questions.

Consequently, I have used reason or intuition to fill in the holes in my life. I have done so with great capacity, and for so long that I am fairly capable of deductive reasoning. The latter maybe the reason I went back to school after seven years to pursuit a master of science in psychology, to hone my skills. But no textbook can have a conversation that two people or a family is long overdue for.

The other option and the one I now choose is to offer forgiveness without having answers. It is more than reasonable to abandon reason for past hurts and move forward with an unburdened purpose towards life together. And since I cannot be absolutely sure of the cause of my pain, or doubt, or fears, then why drag my family into these dark recesses with me. What if neither of us can return the same, or at all? So, I chose the life that stands ahead of me.

I learned the value of acknowledgement in the addiction communities that I have served. My first step is acknowledging that the plan for my life is much bigger than me, and that God is in control of that plan. My second step is acknowledging that no matter my past or present that all things will work together for my good as I am called according to God's purpose. My final step for the moment is to realize that over my shoulder are memories that hurt, but that there are just as many, if not more that make me smile, and laugh, and celebrate. Therefore, I have declared that if rejection was ever an issue for me, and attempted to hold me in the bondage that false evidence presents, that I will forevermore be free from this stigma. I now live free.

Clarence White III is host of Coached 2 Love Radio, which airs every Thursday night at 8:00 p.m. EST on The Survival Radio Christian Network. Tune in live at **www.survivalradiochristiannetwork.com** or call 347-237-4648.

Desire a Purpose Driven Relationship

OMON KENNETH ONI-ESELEH, PH.D

In the beginning, God made the heavens and the earth, day and night, and all the animals on our planet - for a purpose. It is also clear that He made man for a purpose when He declared, let us make in "our own image, according to our likeness"; which symbolizes the need for relationship. Relationship also underscores God's choice of man to name the animals that were first created by Him; and to "let man have dominion over the fish of the sea, over the birds of the air, and over the cattle, over all the earth and over every creeping thing that creeps on the earth" - (Genesis 1:26). It is obvious from scripture that the creation of man by God was purpose driven. However, since Adam and Eve failed the test in the Garden of Eden, man has struggled to maintain a meaningful and lasting relationship with God. As soon as they ate the fruit, they felt different about themselves and their

Maker. They were ashamed of their nakedness and wanted to hide from God. Their innocent, trusting relationship with God vanished. They had knowledge of good and evil, but it was not what they expected. Their ultimate punishment was death: "Humanity henceforth, has been discombobulated, has landed man on a collision course ever since. It did not take Adam's children very long to build or manufacture whatever they needed. They spoke a common language and developed a social structure. They became too independent and too ambitious for their own good. Left to their own self-destructive devices, the children of Adam grew so depraved that God had to send a flood to cleanse the earth and start anew with the family of Noah. Just like their parents, they single-handedly destroyed the personal relationship that existed between them and God."

I am truly convinced that God in His infinite power and ability could have created 10 billion people all at the same time, "in the beginning." God could have created them all the same size, same age, height, etc. However, God chose to create a man and a woman with the divine purpose of procreation. By doing so, God gave man the opportunity to play a role in raising and molding future generations; so that while raising these future generation, man would form relationships, which would allow us to work together as a unit to achieve the same goals and advance our respective societies and the Kingdom of God.

First, a man and a woman would have to develop a purposeful and meaningful relationship; then, they both have to raise their offspring. We then become mentors to our offspring. So, it is clear that God created man with a purpose and initiated the first relationship between man and woman with the utmost purpose of populating the earth and also, for companionship.

Purpose in anything one does in life is the foundation on which success is built. That is how destinies are built. The ability to define, understand and maintain a purpose in life can spell the difference between success and failure in any human venture. It should be noted that relationships could either be permanent or temporary.

An anonymous poet once wrote:

REASON, SEASON, OR LIFETIME:

PEOPLE COME INTO YOUR LIFE FOR A REASON, A SEASON OR A LIFETIME. WHEN YOU FIGURE OUT WHICH ONE IT IS, YOU WILL KNOW WHAT TO DO FOR EACH PERSON.

When someone is in your life for a REASON, it is usually to meet a need you have expressed. They have come to assist you through a difficulty; to provide you with guidance and support; to aid you physically, emotionally or spiritually.

They may seem like a godsend, and they are. They are there for the reason you need them to be.

Then, without any wrongdoing on your part or at an

inconvenient time, this person will say or do something to bring the relationship to an end. Sometimes they die. Sometimes they walk away. Sometimes they act up and force you to take a stand. What we must realize is that our need has been met, our desire fulfilled; their work is done. The prayer you sent up has been answered and now it is time to move on.

Some people come into your life for a SEASON, because your turn has come to share, grow or learn. They bring you an experience of peace or make you laugh. They may teach you something you have never done. They usually give you an unbelievable amount of joy. Believe it. It is real, but only for a season.

LIFETIME relationships teach you lifetime lessons; things you must build upon in order to have a solid emotional foundation. Your job is to accept the lesson, love the person, and put what you have learned to use in all other relationships and areas of your life. It is said that love is blind but friendship is clairvoyant.

— Unknown

Putting this poem in perspective, the questions we are left to answer individually are as follows: are you currently in a relationship either for a season, reason or a lifetime? Do you know the purpose for which you are in any of these relationships?

The purpose for any relationship must be established at

the very beginning of the relationship; not in the middle or much later into the relationship; and there must be an agreement, not necessarily a written agreement, but spiritually and in principle between all parties involved.

One of the most important considerations in establishing a purpose driven relationship is the matching or marrying of visions, dreams, and aspirations in life. To actually establish and maintain a purpose driven relationship and trust its connectivity, accountability and credibility, it is imperative that the parties involved in the relationship have somewhat the same intentions and vision for achieving the ultimate goal. This allows the relationship to be about something greater than just each other, but a common goal that they both are working towards. This works in successful business partnerships and in marriages. When a common mission statement is established, it allows all parties to look at the same goal and purpose as opposed to relying on others for their strength, direction, wisdom, counsel, and insight. It also avoids finger pointing, as all parties involved in the relationship tend to share the blame. In the end, an amicable way of ensuring a lasting, deep, and meaningful purpose driven relationship is to establish and follow a set standard and principles that both parties are committed to living by.

Purpose in this discourse refers to godly purpose; not the worldly purpose that is based on carnality. Take for example, our relationship with God. The Almighty God created man with a purpose. With God, it is our relationship with Him that matters the most, not our titles, not our material possessions, who we are or what we think we are.

The Holy Bible says in 2 Corinthians 6:14, "Do not be yoked together with unbelievers. For what do righteousness and wickedness have in common? Or what fellowship can light have with darkness?"

Some relationships are not worth getting into, and some are not worth mending or maintaining. Some relationships are toxic and destructive. They are not worth latching on to. Know when to cut the cord and let the partner go, rather than try to hold on to them. Abraham had to separate from his nephew Lot before he could receive the abundant blessings God had promised him (Gen. 13:1-18). Jacob faced the same predicament; he had to leave the comfort of his uncle's home with his family, for him to receive the blessings God had lined up for him (Genesis 31:1-21). When such a situation arises, early discernment is key, and courage to call off the relationship. There's always the tendency to want to hold on or give it one more try. The call is yours. You are the quarterback of your own destiny. You may choose to go down on one knee as in a surrender mode, or head for the end zone with the ball and score with it. Remember always, "we are not what happened to us, we are what we wish to become" (Carl G. Jung).

A relationship with no unified purpose needs to be brought

to a necessary ending. It matters not whether it is a business relationship or personal relationship. If the parties involved in the relationship are not working towards a unified goal, there's bound to be a shipwreck. [3] Can two people walk together without agreeing on the direction? (Amos 3:3). A purpose driven relationship is wholesome, not caustic; and it is blameless, without regrets and finger pointing. A purpose driven relationship involves sacrifices on a regular basis. And when is a sacrifice a sacrifice? A sacrifice is a sacrifice when we do things that benefit others at times when we really don't want to do those things. As we are reminded in Philippians 2:5-8 "[5] In your relationships with one another, have the same mindset as Christ Jesus: [6] Who, being in very nature God, did not consider equality with God something to be used to his own advantage; [7]rather, he made himself nothing by taking the very nature of a servant, being made in human likeness.[8] And being found in appearance as a man, he humbled himself by becoming obedient to death, even death on a cross!"

A purpose driven relationship has the following characteristics: honor, mutual respect, love, kindness, compassion, sacrifice, and unity.

The most important relationship man can embark on is a relationship with God. To understand God's purpose, we must understand His Son Jesus and God's purpose for sending His only Son, which is to restore men back into the image of God and ultimately restore His relationship with men, that relationship that was severed when Adam and Eve disobeyed God's command in the Garden of Eden. And that restoration is an ongoing process in the life of a believer. God wants to conform us into the image of Christ if only we will maintain a relationship with Him.

The Kingdom of God is enhanced through relationship building; isolation is not an option. Therefore, believers must desire relationships in order to advance the Kingdom of God. Even earthly relationships advance our society, as no man is an island.

The first institution based on relationship that was ever established by God was marriage between man and woman; and was designed to be sealed with an oath or pledge. It was meant to be lasting and to be the universal symbol and pallbearer for other human relationships. Marriage is a covenanted relationship between a man and a woman. The Bible teaches us in Numbers 30 to obey God's command when we enter into a matrimonial relationship: "This is what the LORD commands: [2] When a man makes a vow to the LORD or takes an oath to obligate himself by a pledge, he must not break his word but must do everything he said.

[3] When a young woman still living in her father's household makes a vow to the LORD or obligates herself by a pledge [4] and her father hears about her vow or pledge but says nothing to her, then all her vows and every pledge by which she obligated herself will stand. [5] But if her father forbids her when he hears

about it, none of her vows or the pledges by which she obligated herself will stand; the Lord will release her because her father has forbidden her. ⁶ If she marries after she makes a vow or after her lips utter a rash promise by which she obligates herself ⁷ and her husband hears about it but says nothing to her, then her vows or the pledges by which she obligated herself will stand. ⁸ But if her husband forbids her when he hears about it, he nullifies the vow that obligates her or the rash promise by which she obligates herself, and the Lord will release her." The relationship between couples should have unconditional commitment if there's to be any future and if set expectations are to be met. So, marriage vows are taken before God and should be taken seriously.

Let me say quickly that the same rules described in the scripture above apply to both men and women. Also, neither the man nor the woman should ever go into a relationship like marriage asking themselves what they would personally benefit from the relationship. They should not go into a marriage relationship thinking if their future spouse would make them happy. Listen to how awkward that sounds; a man thinking if the future wife would make him happy if he stays married to her. And no one already in a relationship should consider leaving because they claim that their spouse no longer makes them happy. That is a selfish, self-centered attitude. The question should be whether you would make your future spouse happy and whether both of you could make the children you bring into this world happy. And if you are already in a relationship and you consider leaving because your spouse no longer makes you happy, the question then will be whether you make her happy?

Really, it should never be about you. Strive to make your partner happy instead. The happiest people are those who put others before themselves. In a godly, purpose driven relationship, you do not give because you expect to receive; you give because you want to give or because it is the right thing to do. "Give, and it shall be given unto you; good measure, pressed down, and shaken together, and running over, shall men give into your bosom. For with the same measure that ye mete withal it shall be measured to you again". - Luke 6:38. This is a spiritual law of giving. So, focus more on giving than receiving.

The purpose of marriage is to unite a man (Husband) and a woman (Wife) together in a covenant relationship with God so that both of them would fulfill God's original plan from creation. "For this reason a man shall leave his father and mother and be joined to his wife, and the two shall become one flesh" (Matthew 19:5). Build your marriage on godly purposes and you will experience the joy and fulfillment of a blissful matrimony.

Marriage is to spiritually and physically unite a man and a woman together as husband and wife; it is a purpose driven relationship between them and God through which God's primary assignment to mankind would be carried out. Therefore, marriage is meant to be a lifetime commitment that we should go into with God's purpose and not carnal, self-centered purpose that breeds fear, pain, tears, frustration, bitterness, regrets, disappointments, and utter failure. Relationships require a lot of work and commitment. If society and ultimately socialization are to survive, it is imperative that we learn to maintain a solid relationship with God and with fellow men. Man has wondered so far from God in search of knowledge, thrills, and wonder. The truth is that, only God is big enough to fill the heart of man with the knowledge, thrills, and wonder that he desperately seeks.

Another important relationship in life is man's relationship with his children. A man's primary purpose or role in the lives of his children is mentorship. Just as Jesus valued the relationship between Him and His father more than anything else, man should value his relationship with his children the same way. We are to love them, protect them, and respect them. "Fathers, do not provoke your children to anger by the way you treat them. Rather, bring them up with the discipline and instruction that comes from the Lord" (Ephesians 6:4).

Ask yourself as a parent a very vital question; in your absence, do you really think that your child would be proud of you or say good things about you to his friends? That could be a true test of your relationship with your child. Therefore, if your relationship with God is fractured, what do you possibly expect God to think of you? If you have ever broken a bone in any part of your body, you would comprehend the fact that, you may will all you want, but it is impossible to move that extremity. Our relationship with God is similar. When our relationship with God is broken, we may will all that we want, it will be impossible to achieve much in life; to ask anything in His name and expect Him to deliver.

My personal relationship with God is the most important of all relationships that I am involved in. I have reached a point in life where I am convinced that without God's grace and His love in my life, I am an empty shell of a being. I owe it all to Him. Get to know Him and experience His love. I had the best of relationships with my earthly parents whom I revered for their mentorship and hands-on parental guidance. My parents also introduced my siblings and me to our Heavenly Father God, with whom we developed a solid relationship very early in our lives. We learned early that, you talk to your children about God when they are young and when they are grown, that is when you talk to God about them. Lessons learned.

Omon Kenneth Oni-Eseleh, Ph.D., is host of The Hour of Victory, which airs every Wednesday night at 7:00 p.m. EST on The Survival Radio Christian Network. Tune in live at www.survivalradiochristiannetwork.com or call 347-237-4648.

The Light

BY J.B. MCGEE

As a Christian, I think of a testimony as a living thing, constantly growing and evolving as we do. We're always going through ups and downs in life, and my experience is that usually it's how I react to the downs that shape my life the most. In fact, it's usually that darkness that leads me into the light, the good times.

I think it's easy to walk by faith when life seems peachy. I also think it's easy to praise God and give Him the glory during those times, but it's when you're in those really difficult places, when it's important to rely on Him the most.

I don't have enough time to tell you my entire testimony, but I want to share with you the last year of my life.

In 2011, we had just moved from our hometown of Aiken, SC, to Atlanta, GA, to be closer to my children's medical team, but also to be in an area with greater mitochondrial disease awareness. What we didn't expect to find out that year was that in addition to me and my children having 'mito,' my husband did, too.

The financial stress of having four chronically ill people in one family had long taken its toll on us. Then there was the stress of also all being sick and being primary caregivers to special needs children. To say that life was overwhelming would be an understatement.

My husband worked in the mortgage loan business. I doubt I need to say more on that to give you any indication as to how our finances had changed in the years leading up to this move. We went from making six figures to living in poverty, and not because we had big flat screen televisions, by taking fancy vacations, or by having luxury vehicles. It was because of the market. And the number one reason in this country for filing bankruptcy, except it costs money to file for bankruptcy, and we didn't even have enough money to do that.

Finances and having a sick child are pretty much at the top of reasons for divorces in this country, too. I had always thought that given what we'd already experienced, we should be able to get through anything. But it seemed in 2011-2012, we just might not be strong enough. A stick can only bend so far before it breaks. My heart felt like it was a sopping wet rag being squeezed dry. I loved my husband so much, but I just wasn't sure that was enough anymore.

So I did my best to keep busy. I kept hearing about *Fifty*

Shades of Grey. Not even knowing it was a book, I put the title into my search box on my computer. One of the first results was for a "Christian" website bashing everything about it. Now if you don't know anything about me, know this: I don't let other people form opinions for me. I want to be educated and form my own opinion. So I downloaded the preview. I thought maybe I could read that and form my opinion. I didn't think of myself as a reader, so I really didn't want to pay for the entire trilogy at thirty dollars, especially when I could barely afford food. When that preview ended, I was left reeling. So that night, I learned how Amazon one-click addictions start.

I stayed up until five o'clock in the morning reading, even though I knew the next day we had an out-of-town doctor's appointment that would last the entire day for both of my children. I had never read anything like that. I felt guilty, yet intrigued. In fact, I didn't put the book away when I left the house. I found myself reading when we'd stop to take restroom breaks. I had trouble putting it down. I had never been so engrossed in a story, well not since the *Left Behind* Series more than ten years ago. This certainly wasn't that. Actually, I worried that reading this book might very well get me left behind.

When I registered my child for his blood work at the doctor's office, the older lady processing our insurance asked me what no one else had. "You aren't reading that *Fifty Shades of Grey*, are you?"

I could feel my cheeks growing rosy. No, they were beyond rosy. They were scarlet. I might as well have had a letter sewn onto my chest, too.

Instead of denying it, I admitted for the first time to a single soul what I was reading. What surprised me the most was that she didn't judge me like I had expected. This being the Bible belt, I had been sure she'd turn her nose up on me, go ahead and brand a letter on my soul with her glare alone, but that didn't happen. She opened up to me. We ended up talking about Jesus, the Bible, and the ways it could be used to bring people closer to Him.

Yes, I just went there.

See, it made me realize so many of the problems in my marriage. I wanted to make it better. I realized the book was fiction, but I also knew that we had experienced that love before. I wanted to reclaim my derailed happily ever after.

So many years I'd spent feeling guilty for even saying the word sex out loud. It wasn't supposed to be like this, was it? It had been hard for me to accept the act as a sacred gift, as something pure and wholesome to be shared with my husband, when for so many years it had been wrong to even talk about it. Furthermore, I was curious. Did people really do this stuff? I felt so naïve. If for nothing else, it was an education on a different culture.

It didn't take me long before feeling like I was cheating on my husband. So, I told him what I'd been reading, and I asked if he'd read it with me. He said no. Ultimately, it wasn't the sex that had me turning the pages. It was the love story.

A story about a man who would do anything for the girl he loved, who adored her. He wanted to please and care for her in every way possible. Isn't that how God intended us to be with our spouse, our soul mate? That was another thing I'd found difficult with marriage. Being a strong-willed, independent girl, I'd really struggled with giving away my control. It had become a joke that I wore the pants in our relationship, even though I knew that wasn't my intended role biblically. Despite this website having said the books were Satan incarnate, I could feel God working through it to guide me to address the problems in my marriage head on.

Except you can't do this when the other person thinks there are no problems. So for months, we struggled. It was like tug of war. I spent many days crying, wishing for the money to get a divorce, or a miracle to save my marriage. Really, I felt so unloved and alone aside from my faith and my relationship with God. I knew there had to be a bigger, better plan for this time of darkness, but I really was very frustrated. It just felt like nothing was going my way, our way.

Books quickly became my medicine. It was an escape from my reality of illnesses, therapies, and stress in general. One day, a story popped into my own mind. It initially was going to be a small part of my personal story, except I got to make people the way I had thought I wanted them to be. I got to alter the ending to my suiting.

I had planned to write erotica, but I quickly found myself trying to find plot twists to get out of writing sex. I felt conflicted because sex was selling, and I had a fan base built of people who shared my love for Fifty Shades, even if only two hundred people. They were excited to read what I was writing. On the other hand, I also had family members begging me to not go there. Ultimately, I decided to write a story that I could live with…a balance, a happy medium.

Once I started writing, it didn't take me long to realize the story that was being translated onto paper was not at all what I had planned or thought it would. It's as if these characters became as real to me as the air I breathed.

During this time, I remember someone close to me telling me that she could feel that the darkness that had shrouded my family was almost over. She knew the light would soon seep into the tunnel. In fact, she reminded me that a tunnel always has a light at the end because if it didn't, it'd be called a cave. We don't go into caves during bad times. We go in tunnels of darkness. They make us stronger, they make us who we are, and they bring us back into the light. They renew and strengthen our relationship with the Lord. They are the foundations of a testimony. I hung onto this theory. Deep down, I could feel it. I knew it, too.

I never gave up during this journey in the darkness or got mad at God. Knowing there was a reason I was going through what I was made it easier to trust what I know to be true: that good comes with every bad.

A song comes to mind; I *Will Praise You in This Storm*. There had been days I had heard it on the radio, and it would bring me to tears. It gave me such comfort and relief. In my book, *Skipping Stones*, one of my favorite quotes is, "If the night ends, there is never a new day. With a new day comes renewed hope, light." It's like God placed this white shawl around my shoulders when I would hear that song, and it drowned out the darkness, even if only temporarily. The light from the sun always makes the darkness vanish.

So back to I *Will Praise You in This Storm*. It talks about the God who gives and takes away. Sometimes it takes us losing material possessions, loved ones, or something that means a lot to us, to appreciate what we're given.

If we've never had something, we don't know to miss it. That's what makes second chances so awesome. We can fully appreciate the new opportunity. For me, I felt like my opportunity at renewed hope was my book. It was written two weeks after I wrote the first word. I had no idea what to do next, so I did what I always do when I don't know the answers.

I went to the University of Google like I had done a few months earlier to learn about *Fifty Shades of Grey*, when I needed to understand medical stuff in a language and on a level I understood, or when I wanted to learn how to run my own business. I had always been someone to just figure it out.

I think I get that ability from my father; he's a jack-of-all-trades. There's not much he doesn't know how to do. I was also pretty sure there wasn't much he wouldn't do for his little girl, either. He'd all but told me he wished he could make my situation better.

So, of course, like any little girl who wants something does, I called Dad. I'd really rehearsed my speech. I'd also done some crunching numbers. Like some entrepreneurs prepare to go on the television show *Shark Tank*, I'd prepared for the only investor I had the courage to go before to ask for more money. I valued my company, which wasn't much. This was a deal that relied on faith, hope, trust, and most of all love. I said, "I know you're not rich. I know times are tough. I know I should be asking for grocery money instead of money to edit this crazy book I wrote. But can I borrow some money?"

At the time, I had two hundred Facebook likes on my author page. There were another three thousand on my fan page called *For the Love of Fifty Shades of Grey*. My best friend had told me to join a book club several weeks before as a way to talk with other women who were maybe going through similar struggles. Leaving my husband and children for any length of time was not an option, and driving to a book club would cost gas money. I didn't have any. So this page had become my book club. These strangers quickly became good friends, and they gave me the support and encouragement I needed.

So when I was doing my number crunching, I thought if just

half of the people on my author page, people who had already expressed interest in the book, bought a copy, I'd be able to pay him back.

In my research on Google, I knew that as a self-published author, I could call myself successful if I sold more than two hundred fifty copies. So I tried hard to keep my dreams in check. I kept telling myself that I would not be the next E.L. James, the author of *Fifty Shades of Grey*, but I knew she'd had to start somewhere. I've always been an optimist, one to reach for the stars. There was always a glimmer of hope, always a ray of light that maybe this was it for me.

On September 29, 2012, with the help of my father, I published my first book, *Broken*. I sold thirty copies in the first day. The reviews were pretty decent. I watched that rank on Amazon climb. Before long, I noticed it was hanging out with books I had read and loved. That was surreal. Then, a Facebook page I knew and had dreamed about being featured on, *What to Read After Fifty Shades of Grey*, started sharing my book. I couldn't believe it, probably because it wasn't even erotica. They didn't care. People didn't seem to care. They bought it up, and they were reading it. Each day, new likes appeared on my Facebook page. New messages started coming in from complete strangers having the reaction to my book that was familiar. It was the reaction I had been having to all of these other books I had recently read.

One of the messages was from Michelle Eck. It was a pivotal

moment not only in my life, but also in my career as an author. Not only did she live nearby, she also had been on a street team that had helped propel one of my other favorite authors into stardom. And she wanted to help little ol' me. When I asked her what I owed her for helping me, she basically told me that making sure my family would be okay was payment enough. She didn't even know me.

I'll never forget the day she told me to get a new *professional* author picture. My neighbors treated me like a rock star, doing hair, makeup, and they even took the pictures because I was so broke I couldn't afford a professional photographer. Heck, they even told me what to wear. I would have never paired green on green the way they did. But it worked.

Black Friday came. I had started to make friends in this Indie world of books. People were asking to interview me. There was a blog tour, which is an online book tour. Walking the streets of downtown Aiken with my best friend, the one who told me to join a book club, I remember constantly refreshing my numbers on Amazon. I watched them soar to the top. She laughed, "This wasn't exactly what I meant when I said join a book club, you know?" We giggled like we used to do in the good old days. She told me, "Just think. Maybe this time next year, you'll be signing books on Black Friday." That was another goal, another dream, and it seemed that God was on a roll making mine finally come true.

By Christmas, I remember being glued to my computer during my holiday as the second book, *Mending*, was released. The numbers constantly multiplied. I had my first book signing in my hometown, and was featured in the local newspaper. A few weeks later, I was propelled into being a best-selling author in what seemed like the blink of an eye.

I wish I could say that my marriage was perfect by then, and that all of the previous problems in my life were just as easily resolved, but they weren't. Things were still really rough in my personal life. It wasn't until February, right after my third book, *Conspiring*, was published that things changed.

For me, my health deteriorated. The work that I *wasn't* supposed to be doing coupled with the constant emotional stress induced a crisis from the mitochondrial disease. I ended up having to have a port put in for IV fluids, and I spent about 6 weeks in the bed trying to recover. *This*, I think, is when my marriage started to get better.

My husband watched me fall apart, and there was nothing he could do to put me back together. I think we both realized that we couldn't live this life without each other, and we both needed to be well. We devised a plan to try to keep me healthy and writing, which at this point was paying nearly all of our bills. Our house in South Carolina had been near foreclosure, but we were able to save it. Our car that we were about to lose because of a desperate title loan was paid off. We felt slowly, but surely, the bricks that had been suffocating our spirits were lifting.

One day, Chad, my husband, asked me to go on a picnic to Lake Lanier. I watched him skip stones with my boys – well at least try to teach them to skip stones. That's when I really knew I was in the light, at least until our next episode of darkness. I'd be foolish to think there wouldn't be anymore.

A story, *Skipping Stones*, was born. I had to finish *Forgiven* before I could start writing it. Writing *Forgiven* was cathartic in so many ways for me. I had a lot of forgiving to do with my marriage, with my family, and with a lot of experiences that had previously kept me in the darkness.

While *Skipping Stones* hasn't become a *New York Times* or *USA Today* best seller like I had hoped it would, someone once told me that numbers don't always measure success.

Success is measured by the impact the story has on other people's hearts, and in the case of this book, it was a success. Maybe that's because it's so personal. It's about nearly losing it all and surviving.

I am not rich, we're still sick, but we're extremely blessed. Last June, God started setting up this moment and the opportunity for me to have a ministry of my own. I am not going to lie. It scares me. That's a big responsibility, but I know that I can't ignore the call.

I'm not perfect, none of us are. I don't regret one single thing I've done so far, and I know I'll mess up along the way here or there, but I will never give the devil the satisfaction of denouncing my great God.

It's the times in the darkness that bring us into the light. It's the times the devil tries to make us question God that bring us closer to the Holy Spirit. So given the opportunity to rewrite my story, making up my ending, isn't quite as appealing. Doing that would alter my testimony, making me weaker than I already am. Instead, I've decided to use my experiences for good.

Black Friday of 2013, I signed books in my hometown bookstore. I'm writing my sixth novel, *Saving Alex*, represented by Donaghy Literary Group, and am host of a Christian radio show, *The Light with J.B. McGee*. And it's all because of a book that a Christian blog denounced called *Fifty Shades of Grey*. There is always good in the bad, hope in the hopeless.

May we always find light in the darkness.

J.B. McGee is host The Light with J.B. McGee, which airs every Monday night at 8:30 p.m. EST on The Survival Radio Christian Network. Tune in live at **www.survivalradiochristiannetwork.com** or call 347-237-4648.

Transformation

BY JOHNNETTE YOUNG

Labored breathing and clammy hands, head feeling as though it had been stricken by a five pound bag of quarters, and my uniform sweat soaked, from fear of the unknown consequences that lie just before me. Should I keep running or should I stop? "Six easy steps to the door marked exit to your left", came a voice from deep within me. I dropped to my knees crying silently and praying. It's the only thing I could do; my feet were heavy, as though they were set in a block of dried cement. "God, please help me, I don't know what to do, I am so tired; I am weak and need your strength, please guide me, please, Father, just guide me, I'm so tired I can't do this anymore, please take over." I welcomed the cool breeze that came over me, drying the sweat that beaded my face and arms. I felt a sudden peace envelop my body and immediately relax my tensed muscles. The pain that had been pounding like a drum inside my head gently subsided, and my breathing leveled out to a normal rhythm. I took a deep breath, rose from my knees and stepped out into plain view of the two awaiting detectives and hotel security. "Please step into the office, Ms. Walters, I am Detective Iverman, and this is Detective Branson. We are trying to figure out who you are, Ms. Walters." says Det. Iverman. "What do you mean?" I asked. "Look," says Det. Branson, "We can do this the easy way, or we can do it the hard way." Once again, I took a deep breath and relaxed. "My name is Johnnette Odella Young, and I am a fugitive from Plainfield, New Jersey." The words came easy, as if I had recited them a million times in my head, and with them came a sense of peace that I had never felt before in my life. I exhaled a sigh of relief; the weight of the world had been lifted from my shoulders in that very moment. Det. Iverman spoke first, "Fair enough, Ms. Young" with a look of sympathy on his face. I bowed my head, thanking God for arresting me, for arresting me spiritually. Nothing could match the spiritual torment that I was feeling; going to jail was the easy part. I walked out of the hotel that I'd worked in for 3 weeks with the detectives close behind. They refused to put handcuffs on me; it was as if they could sense that I was tired of running as well.

With that arrest, a new chapter in my journey through life began. At the police station, I made my one phone call, which was to my mother. When she answered the phone, the first words out of my mouth were "Ma, it's over." in a relieved tone. She responded, "Thank God, what can I do to help you?" I said, "Please, come and get my baby." Tears were flowing, and I had a huge lump in my throat from striving not to cry. I didn't want her worrying any more than she already was. That day I was charged with Identity Theft; I used a family member's name to secure employment at a prestigious hotel that was located in the city that I was currently living in. The charge was of low degree because I wasn't using her social security number, I made one up. Detective Iverson contacted New Jersey to inform them that he had me in custody. This began the extradition process of the New Jersey Task Force coming to Pennsylvania to get me. I was taken to the county prison to await an upcoming court date.

Once I was in the county prison, I started thinking about the amount of time I would have to serve before I could be with my children again. When this ordeal began, I left my then six year old son with my family to care for; being on the run with a six year old child would have been just plain wrong. He deserved better than that. Eighteen months after I left home, I gave birth to my second child; at the time of my arrest she was only seven and a half weeks old. Know and understand that I felt like the worst mother ever. There were so many things running through my mind that I couldn't focus on any single one for more than ten seconds. Depression weighed upon me heavily that evening. I spoke with God in depth that evening, with as much sincerity and conviction as I could muster, and asked for His help in guiding me through the hell that I had created for myself. I laid atop a gym mat that was placed on a metal bunk bed that night and, as uncomfortable as it was, I fell into a deep sleep and dreamed of the circumstances that had taken place that landed me in this awful place that would be my dwelling for the next three months and ten days. I was then extradited to Elizabeth, New Jersey's Union County Jail for two months, then to Delaney Hall, which is an in-house alternative to jail facility for eight months until I went to court for prison sentencing. In May of 2002, I was sentenced to three years of state prison at the Edna Mahan Correctional Facility for Women. At the time of my sentencing, my relationship with God was better than any other time in my life. Clearly, I didn't like the fact that I had to do three years of prison, but I was okay, because I knew that I would not be doing this time alone. I had a supreme guide to assist me along my journey; I had God and He was lived inside of me. I also had a divine manual, which was my bible, the living word of God. I was straight, and I was ready; all praises due to God, I was ready.

The jail time I did prior to being sentenced was credited to the three years that I had served in state prison. I was released in July of 2004, and was back in Pennsylvania on the verge of a new beginning. While I was locked up, my mother suffered a massive stroke and ended up in a nursing home. My mother was the primary care giver for my little lady so Children and Youth Services ended up taking custody of her; my son was in New Jersey with other family. Children and Youth Services would not give her to me immediately because I had just come home from prison. To make a long story short, I jumped through hoops and barrels to get her back, and I did it in a matter of months. She was three years old at this time, and there was a lot of catching up that we had to do.

When I came home, I had no money and no viable resources that I could get help from, except welfare. When I had gotten locked up back in 2001, the hotel manager told me that she was so sorry that I had to go through what I was going through because I was such a good person. She told me that when I got out I could have my job back if I needed it. Well, she made good on that offer, and I got my job back. My job, along with welfare benefits, helped, but I needed more. I would go to church and pray for some sort of breakthrough. I never doubted that one would come; I just didn't know how it would come, or even how to make it happen. The re-entry programs that the county had for female ex-offenders were a joke, I was maintaining better on what I was doing on my own. I held a housekeeper position at the Hilton for over a year. The slow season had arrived and hours were being cut tremendously, so I was forced to take another job. I needed money badly, bills were piling up, and I needed to move my son down from New Jersey to be with me and his sister. I needed my family together and I was willing to work as hard as I needed to make that happen. I started doing temp jobs. They would last anywhere from three weeks to six months. It was work, but temping was not a good cycle to be on. I wanted so much out of life. I would just bow my head and pray at times, didn't matter where I was, I'd just do it and ask God to help me to keep it movin'.

While I was in prison, I was in a program for thirteen months. While there, one of the counselors thought that I'd be a good candidate for a program named Project Pride. Myself and four other ladies would go on trips to colleges, schools, youth programs, and juvenile detention centers under the supervision of correctional officers to share our experiences, in hopes to deter them from following in our footsteps. I loved being a part of Project Pride for two reasons. One reason was because I had the opportunity to help others. The second was because I got to eat food from the outside world. While I was participating in this program, God moved on me. It was like He was tapping me on my shoulder saying, "This is it, this is what I called you to do." But when I came home, I had no idea on how to make it happen. I thought I needed money, and lots of it, so that
dream was put on the backburner.

I continued to do temp jobs as my means for money and got into a relationship. I became pregnant with the last child that I would give birth to. The relationship was extremely rocky, and I knew in my heart that it wouldn't last. I guess you could say that I was pretty much going through the motions. I was so ready to move onto something bigger and much better than the mediocre lifestyle that I was currently living. I tried hard to get a decent paying job, to no avail. Rent was due and I was about to be evicted from the house that we were living in. My significant other was from Pittsburgh, and he suggested that we go stay with his mother until we got on our feet. I agreed, thinking that anything was better than the current situation that we were in. Well he had gotten into some trouble, so I ended up going before him. I took a bus to Pittsburgh a week later. It was about 10:00 pm when my little lady and I arrived in the city. I was pregnant with my son, and very irritable from the uncomfortable ride. The very first building that I noticed was the UPMC Steel Tower. I remember saying to myself, "I bet the people who work in that building make a lot of money, and I wish I was one of them, ha, wouldn't that be something." Life was extremely hectic in Pittsburgh for a while. I moved back to Harrisburg for a few months and gave birth, then moved back to Pittsburgh. His dad and I broke up shortly after he turned one year old, and that was that. I had a whole lot of ups and downs, but then came my breakthrough!

I used welfare as a temporary support system for me and my little people. I couldn't get a decent job because of my background. It happened on a Thursday at 3:30 a.m. I was sitting in front of an old computer that I purchased from Goodwill for $80. I was on a job search engine putting in applications. I was so tired of not getting hired for jobs, or getting hired but not being able to start the job because of my background; it was horrible. Once again, I bowed my head to my Father God and asked for guidance. A voice from deep within me said, "Just stop." And I did just what it said. I stopped job searching and began living my dream which I came to realize was actually my divine purpose in life. "I am a speaker, and I'm gonna claim it!" were the words that I had spoken out loud. I saved up some of the money that I was getting from welfare, along with money that I had previously saved, and formed my own business. Serene Motivations, LLC was a gift from God. He gave me the gift of voice, and I had more than enough experiences in my life that could keep me talking for a very long time.

Today, I am a Transformational Speaker and author. I provide solutions to reduce welfare recidivism and correctional recidivism for women and youth. I am also the host of Serene Motivations radio on the Survival Radio Christian Network. I thank God without ceasing for ordaining these platforms for me to share the wisdom of my journeys, to be a guide in educating others on how to live unlimited spiritually, mentally and physically. It's a divine blessing to be able to do this using the word of God. I strive to assist as many people as I can in building a powerful, steadfast relationship with God as I can. It's a true pleasure to be able to serve such a mighty God.

As I stand in front of an audience of 47 women, I start my presentation as such, "In January of 1999, I was involved in a drug raid. Union County Drug Task Force executed a warrant for my cousin, who was a so called big time drug dealer. At the time that this warrant was being executed, he was not on the premises, but I was, along with one of his drug runners. I was arrested and charged with everything that this runner had. If you get caught in a raid, you're going down along with everybody else. I chose to keep my mouth shut and not tell anything. I was living by the so-called code of the streets, "If it happens in the streets, it stays in the streets." I believed that if I had said anything that my life may be taken anyway. I wasn't selling drugs, but I was still there in the presence of those who were selling, so that made me just as guilty as them. I went to jail, got bailed out, and was on the run for 18 long months, away from my children, family, and friends, and at times homeless and hungry. Is that the type of life you want to live? If not, then listen up! Cause I got some thangs to tell ya!"

I absolutely love the life that I am living today! I am no longer maintaining; I am truly living a wonderful, fulfilling, and joyful life as a Christian. And that tower of a building that I saw some years back when I first rode into the city of Pittsburgh on the bus, that building is now home for my business, Serene Motivations, LLC! Thank you so very much, Father God, for your loving grace and mercy. I am truly grateful to have been arrested by God.

Johnnette Young is co-host along with Terrelle Lewis of Serene Motivations with, which airs every Wednesday morning at 11 a.m. EST on The Survival Radio Christian Network. Tune in live at **www.survivalradiochristiannetwork.com** or call 347-237-4648.

Love Doesn't Hurt

BY JOYCE WHITE

Love is the greatest gift. 1 Corinthians 13:4-8 states that love suffers long and is kind; love does not envy; love does not parade itself; is not puffed up; does not behave rudely, does not seek its own, is not provoked, thinks no evil; does not rejoice in iniquity, but rejoices in the truth; bears all things, believes all things; hopes all things; endures all things. Love never fails. Many people grow up in families that don't show love, and they wind up choosing the wrong mate to share their life with. I am someone who wasn't shown love as a child. My parents only bought myself and my older siblings' things to meet and exceed our needs. Trying to think back to my childhood, I cannot remember my parents ever telling me that they loved me. As a family, we never showed each other affection. But what my parents did show me was anger and strict discipline, which involved harmful words and lots of spankings. It seems that all my mom ever did was yell and cuss at us for every little thing we did that was not pleasing to her. Then, my dad would be the one who would always spank us for not getting our homework correct, staying outside past seeing the street lights come on, and when we acted up around the house. I used to say that if they ever got divorced that I would go and live with my grandmother in New Jersey, because they were just too strict and darn right mean. Then, as I became a teenager, around fourteen years old, my mother was diagnosed with cancer because she smoked frequently. At one point, I thought she was getting better and that everything would be alright. See, in my family, since we did not communicate, I had no idea what my mom was going through. Then one day, she had gotten sick to the point that she needed to be taken to the hospital. I can't recall how many times I was allowed to visit her, but I do recall the morning that I found out she had passed away. It was on May 28, 1980. I was fifteen years old, and woke up that morning, headed downstairs, and saw my dad and grandmother in the kitchen. I could feel heaviness among them. So when I asked my dad why he did not wake me up to go to school, that is when he shared the news with me of my mother passing away the night before. I still get choked up when having to relive the memory. My mother passed away, and I was not able to tell her goodbye. But I know that from heaven she knows that I love and miss her dearly. After her funeral, my father became much nicer. He found a better job in Colorado with the Food and Drug Administration. But my sister and I still had one more year left in high school. He made the decision to ask his older sister Mary to come and live with us until we graduated in June of 1982. At that point, I was struggling to cope with the loss of my mother and the fact that my dad was no longer cracking the whip on me. So that is when I started making bad choices when it came to dating, or finding someone to be in a relationship with. My parents weren't there for me to teach me to respect myself enough not to just settle for any man or to value my body like the Bible states. So I ended up falling for the nice looking light skinned man who did not know how to respect or treat a woman. Not to mention that I had a thing for guys that needed assistance. I guess my need to take care of people is where that came from, and I thought that I could fix them. For thirty one years, I have gone through relationship after relationship, never finding that special person that God has intended for me to spend the rest of my life with. The first time I fell in love was at the age of 17, or I thought it was love. We met at an apartment complex during the summer of 1981. I was visiting my current boyfriend who lived a few doors down from him. Ended up going to the swimming pool and that's when I saw him. Cute and light skinned, not knowing that he was all wrong for me. I call that my young and dumb moment. We dated for eight years, and he is the father of my son and daughter.

I believe the reason that our relationship failed was that he was not shown love as a child, just like I wasn't. So we were two unloved people coming together trying to have a relationship. His father was not a good example for him to follow, because he was unfaithful to his wife. So, as they say, the apple does not fall far from the tree. Now here comes a lesson for all the women out there looking for that one man God has intended for you. We need to be careful with how we choose a mate. What looks good on the outside is not always good for us in the long run. We have to see where his mind is, and if he is truly allowing God to lead him. I am not saying that we have to choose a man that is not pleasing to our eyes, but like it says in the Bible, we must be equally yoked. What I mean is that you and your mate should first both be believers and have the same mindset when it comes to dealing with life's challenges. Now, all that I am sharing with you comes from personal experience. I promised myself that one day I would sit down and write about my struggles to find the man God intends for me to spend the rest of my life with. I see so many young ladies involved with the wrong type of guy, and I just want to do my part to help this younger generation thrive. Sometimes I feel that if I kept God first back when I was a teenager, then half of what I went through would have never occurred. But then again, God knows my beginning all the way to my end. He has ordered my steps and everything that has occurred in my relationships, whether good or bad, are all a part of his plan for my life. For your tests make up your testimonies. No test, no testimonies. After I finally decided to leave my children's father alone, due to his constant deceit, I kept on finding other light skinned men who weren't right for me, but because they looked good and made me feel good, I allowed them to stay in my life. Also, I forgot to mention that I am a people pleaser, giver, and never wanted anyone to dislike me. So I feel that guys could see that in me, and would think that they could just take advantage of me and I would accept it. But I am not putting all the blame on the men, because I allowed it to happen for the longest time. It took me until the beginning of 2013 to realize that I keep on choosing the wrong type of man due to always being attracted to the fine gentleman, instead of the average guy, who has more to offer then good looks and great sex. Oh yes, not only did they have to be good looking, muscular, and average height. They also had to be good in bed. I believe I used sex to feel loved. Remember, my parents never told me they loved me, nor did they show me any affection. So I used sex to fill that void. I am here to tell you that sex is not the answer when you are not feeling loved. Now most relationships are based on sex first and everything else comes after that. I am not going to lie, I have slept with people on the first date and then never spoke to them again. But we should value our bodies as temples. Keeping them Holy and acceptable unto the Lord. As adults, we should be teaching this to our children, instead of allowing them to learn about it on television or from another peer. Having lost my mother at the age of 15, I was never told anything about sex, so I learned about it on my own. This is how I ended up with two babies by the time I was 20 year old. Luckily, I had my father to help me with raising them. One day, I decided that I would give my children's father an ultimatum. He would have to start sending me money, or he could help me by taking one of his kids with him to live, so it would ease my burden of not having enough money to support them. He decided to take the oldest my daughter back with him to Georgia. At that time I was living in Maryland. I had not planned on allowing him to keep her forever, just long enough for me to get my finances in order. She was only with him for about 6 months before I decided to move back to Georgia in order to be a family with him and our children. So I thought. What actually ended up happening was that he lied to me about being a family. Turns out that he was already dating someone else and tried to maintain that lie after my son and I drove all the way down to Georgia from Maryland. At that time, I was living with his parents, since I could not afford a place on my own. Once I learned that he was seeing someone else, I no longer wanted to be around him, so I found a roommate and moved out of his parent's house. I also left my son and daughter with him, since I could not afford a place on my own. After living with a young lady who I had never met before and we were not really getting along too well, I went looking for a reasonably priced one bedroom apartment and promised myself that I would never live with someone as a roommate ever again. And as of today, I have never broken that promise. I did allow two guys to stay with me briefly. But that situation did not work out, because they did not work nor contributed anything to the household. This goes to show you that one person doing everything in a relationship is really not a relationship. I call that a one-person-ship. You have heard the saying, it takes two to tango. Well, it takes two people working together to make a relationship thrive. Each person must be willing to communicate, lift up one another when things go wrong, not be judgmental, or tear someone down mentally. You should feel safe telling that person your dreams, passions, and goals, along with your thoughts and feelings. I believe the biggest mistake being made in relationships is that we tend to rush the getting to know a person stage. We are so happy and infatuated with a person when we first meet that we ignore the warning signs that come around and let us know that this person really should not be in our lives. Not realizing that the longer you stay in an unhealthy relationship, feelings will develop, and then it will be harder to walk away. You start telling yourself that you can deal with craziness your partner is displaying. Speaking from experience, you should just muster up enough courage and tell that person respectfully that you all should go your separate ways. It won't be easy at first, but time heals all wounds. The key to healing from a break up is to keep an open and clear mind. Try not to hold onto anger, unforgiveness, and bitterness, because you will carry that into your next relationship. For the Bible says that unforgiveness is spiritual poison. It is the most popular poison that the enemy uses against God's people, and one of the deadliest poisons a person can take spiritually. It causes everything from mental depression, to health problems such as cancer and arthritis. Not saying that every single case of cancer is due to unforgiveness, but cancer can develop if you keep unforgiveness in your heart. Cancer comes from the devil. Doctors don't understand where it comes from; it's the symptoms of a curse. Jesus gave us very important commandments to follow; one of them was to love one another, as he loved us (John 15:12). Love is the exact opposite of unforgiveness, envy, jealousy, hate, pride, and bitterness. You can't truly love somebody and hold bitterness or unforgiveness against him or her at the same time. Here are a few negative effects of unforgiveness: it shows you don't really love Jesus, it prevents God from forgiving our sins, opens us up to the tormentors (The Devil), blocks God from answering our prayers, can defile a person, gives Satan an advantage, can keep a person out of heaven, can prevent us from being fruitful spiritually, and opens us up to curses. Here are the positive effects of forgiveness: it opens us up to God's forgiveness, puts us in a receiving position when we pray, it helps us become spiritually fruitful, and we are reconciled with our Heavenly Father when we love each other. So forgiveness is a magnificent blessing! Now I want to share a story with you about an abusive relationship I found myself in when I was in my late 20's. We met in a night club, and he approached me after watching me from across the room. He asked me to dance, and seemed like a nice guy, but again I was looking only at his outward appearance. As the night progressed, we laughed and had a great time. He asked me for my phone number, and I gave it to him, when it was time for us to go our separate ways. We began calling each other and then started hanging out together. As I got to know him, I found out that he had moved here from Mississippi and was staying with his older sister. He really did not have a job, so his sister let him work at the TCBY store where she was a manager. Since it was in my nature to be a caring person who always looked out for someone in need, I allowed him to move in with me. That's when the abuse started. He would punch me whenever I said or did something that made him mad, and then would try and smooth it over with an apology. At that time, I didn't think highly of myself, since I was still trying to get over the break up and deceit from my children's father. So I accepted his mistreatment, and even thought that I brought the beatings on myself because I was a bad person. Later on, he shared with me that his father would beat his mother, and that is why he acted that way. So instead of leaving him, I would take pity on him, and try to be understanding of his faults. But here is a side note ladies. If a man has grown up seeing abuse from his relatives, then chances are he will become abusive towards you, because it has become part of who he is. That is something you can't help him with. He has to break that curse. So at the first signs of anger, verbal abuse, bitterness, and wanting to control your life, please do not remain with that person. They are not the one for you, and God would never send someone to you to cause you pain and mental anguish. Here are some examples of the kind of abuse he inflicted on me. One night, while we were outside, he hit me right in my eye with my glasses on, and I received small cuts over my right eye. I still have a slight scar over my eye to remind me of that night. He also held an unloaded gun to my head, kicked me and caused my head to hit the dresser, and almost smothered me to death with a pillow. There was one time when I fought back. We were sitting in my car talking, and I was expressing my feelings about how he hurt me. Then, all of a sudden, out of anger I put my hands around his neck, and started choking him to the point where he couldn't breathe. That was my breaking point, and after that, we broke up and went our separate ways. Years later, I think I ran into his sister, and she told me that he had moved back to Mississippi and I can't tell you how much relief I felt, knowing that I would never run into him again.

The next guy I met was half Puerto Rican and half African American. We met at an apartment complex while I was visiting a good friend of mine helping her move. He seemed nice too, but again, I was looking at his appearance. After getting to know him, I found out that his mother was a prostitute and that is how he was born. Plus he wasn't stable and needed assistance. Once again, my need to assist kicked in, and I allowed him to live with me. This had become a pattern for me, but at that time, I couldn't see it. I only wanted to be loved, and had no idea what love really is. After we broke up, I made a conscious decision to never allow a man to live with me again until we got married, no matter how needy he was. Of course, that decision did not stick, because when I was attending church, I met another man who was very handsome, and acted like he had it all together. I thought that I was taking my time with this one, and that God had sent him my way. But because this guy knew the Bible real well and called himself a minister, I let my guard down and was tricked by his kind words. This is why we should read and know the Bible for ourselves, so we won't be tricked by the enemy. With this guy, I actually intended to marry him. But I thank God that I never went through with it. He was a recovering crack addict, and he would have relapses from time to time. I gave him my support, prayers, love, forgiveness, and even bailed him out of jail. We also ended up living together for a short period of time. Once I gained the courage to let him go because it was obvious that the help he needed I could not provide, I totally rededicated my life to Christ and started to attend church regularly. Later on, I would discover that the Devil knows your weaknesses. One of the ways that the Devil gets me off track with my walk with God is to send good looking men with muscles my way, and they cause me to turn away from the church. Without fail, I would always give in to temptation, and allow them to push God second, when God should always be first. The last time this happened was in 2007 when I met a guy online. But this guy wasn't the normal type I had been attracted to. Guess I decided to switch things up, and seek to know the person's heart instead of his outward appearance. The first time we met in person was for dinner. He had good conversation, and he was the first guy that actually took care of me. We actually developed a great friendship, and I would spend all my free time with him. Later on, he would introduce me to his mother and grandmother. Since I did not have close family here in Georgia, he offered his family to me. I thought that was very kind of him. He showed me how to cook and respected me as a person. But because he had issues with God not helping him when he was younger, while his mom was involved in an abusive relationship, and the fact that his brother was a diabetic, I allowed him to pull me out of the church once again. For some reason, I tend to follow the ways of people, no matter if it is negative or if it is positive. One of my nicknames is

Chameleon, because I can change my mood or attitude to fit any situation. I really prefer to keep a positive outlook on things because it is better for your spirit. Our friendship lasted for 6 years, but what made me decide that it was time to end our friendship was realizing that his negative spirit was killing my positive spirit, and that the kind of help he needed I could not provide. We had promised to stay friends forever, but people are put in our lives for a reason, season, or lifetime. His season was over, especially when every time we spoke he would leave me feeling very angry, instead of uplifted. I felt that God was telling me this person is no longer fit to be in your life, because I have greater things for you, and he will only keep you bound and confused. Now, he did not take it well, and ended up throwing things about me that I shared with him back in my face. In other words, he truly showed me the type of person that he really was. I mean, he once shared with me that a woman in California came up to him and told him that he has an evil spirit on him. Why, when I heard that I did not take it as a sign that this guy is trouble and that I should really leave him alone and just pray for him. Sometimes that is why God may put certain people in your path to pray for them and keep moving on. One of my mottos I now try to incorporate in my life is to Live, Love, and Laugh, and if someone is grieving my spirit, then I tell them no harm, but I have to keep it moving. Life is too short, and we need to do whatever it takes to keep our mind, body and spirit well.

God has allowed all of these experiences in my life to mold and shape me into the person that I am now. I may not understand why all of this has happened to me, but I thank God that he loves me so much and will not let any harm, hurt, or danger befall me. I will end my chapter with a prayer: *Now our Lord Jesus Christ himself, and God, even our Father, which hath loved us, and hath given us everlasting consolation and good hope through grace, Comfort your hearts, and establish you in every good word and work. 2 Thessalonians 2:16, 17*

Joyce White is host of Faith Walk with Joyce White, which airs every Tuesday night at 7:30 p.m. EST on The Survival Radio Christian Network. Tune in live at **www.survivalradiochristiannetwork.com** or call 347-237-4648.

I Was Born For This

BY JOY MARINO

I cannot be late for this audition. I have waited my entire life for this opportunity and nothing can keep me from it. Who shows up late, for a date with destiny? Prayerfully it will not be me. This is my destiny... isn't it? Well, I believe that it is. I know the doors God opens, no man can shut. And what is for me is for me...right? I promise I do not doubt Your word. I just need a little blessed assurance. Not that You have to explain anything. But, I really would like to know. Please speak to me Lord.

The phone rang. *Wow, that was fast.* "Hello?"

"Sunshine, thank God you are okay."

"Umm yeah... why wouldn't I be?"

"There was a shooting, about ten minutes ago, right next door to your audition."

"Well you don't have to worry about me. I am sitting in

traffic as we speak."

"For once, I am happy that you are running late."

"Lacey, I am usually on time so don't try to play me like I'm not. I am not going to focus on your sarcasm. I am just going to thank God for preserving my life. See all things do work out for our good because we love Him and are called according to His purpose."

"Slow your role. You have not arrived there yet. There are a million things that could still go wrong."

"Lacey, do you hear yourself right now? Why are you being so negative? What happened to your faith?"

"I am not negative, just realistic. And it has nothing to do with my faith or a lack thereof."

"Well regardless of what you think, God's got this. I left my house an hour and a half earlier than I needed just to make sure I would not be late. But I still am not there. Why do you think that is?"

"I have no idea."

"Clearly God delayed me, to keep me! Do you really think He'd do all of that for nothing?"

"I have no idea. Look, I believe in God, too, but believing everything will always work out, just seems like crap to me. And what happens if it doesn't?"

"Then I would still trust Him."

"Sunshine, you sound fanatical."

"Maybe, I do but it still isn't going to change who I am or

my purpose in life. I was born for this!"

"What if you weren't? I mean there are millions of little girls who wake up every day from a dream very similar. But the key is they wake up. They are not dreaming well into their forties. They get over it and get real jobs."

"Lacey, I am a high powered attorney so I have a real job. I just never gave up on my dreams. God says to write the vision and make it plain. I wrote it down and plainly see myself on the big screen."

"And that was okay to believe as a child, but as a grown woman? Sounds strange to me…where are you?"

"Are you serious right now? First, you belittle my faith and dreams, and then try to act concerned? Honestly, I don't have a clue where I am. Hold on let me see."

"I am not belittling your faith or your dreams. I am simply trying to be your voice of reason."

"The only voice I need to listen to concerning this situation is God's. I am turning onto Peachtree Road now."

"Peachtree goes on forever. What's around you?"

"I don't know. I just passed Diddy's restaurant."

"Are you headed north or south?"

"I think south. The GPS is telling me to take the ramp onto James Wendell George Pkwy in a few miles. It looks like it's putting me back onto I-75."

"Sunshine I don't think you are going to make it."

"Cancel those words! Oh my goodness. Why would you

speak negatively about this? I am going to make it!"

"I am not being negative I am being realistic."

"Lacey, ughh...! Tell me why we are friends again?"

"We are friends because I bring you back down to earth. You are always happy, upbeat, and positive."

"Wow, so you admit that you are negative?"

"Yes, but I called to check on you didn't I?"

"Yes, Lacey. That was very positive of you."

"Now, who is being sarcastic?"

"Lacey that wasn't sarcasm. I am being very sincere. Hold on let me call you back. This guy is motioning for me to roll down my window."

"Don't, Sunshine, people are crazy. Just keep driving and don't let ..." Sunshine ended the call and pulled off to the side of the road. She let down her window.

"Excuse me, ma'am, but my car just died, my cell phone died, I am running late and I really need a ride."

"I am sorry sir but I am not trying to be the next thing to die. I can call you a cab. But since the state of Georgia does not allow me to carry my concealed weapon; and I don't know you from Adam, I'll have to say no."

"I understand." The stranger laughed. "If you have a license to carry, maybe I'm the one who should be afraid?"

"I'm already running late. I honestly don't know why I stopped." Sunshine's phone rang. She noticed it was Lacey, and ignored the call.

"You stopped because I prayed."

"Excuse me what did you just say?"

"I said I prayed. So when you stopped, I assumed you were the answer to that prayer. Then again, a pistol packing woman, wasn't what I'd expected either."

"You know what get in." The phone rang again. It was Lacey again. Sunshine ignored it as the stranger entered her baby blue Jaguar.

"Thank you so much! God is going to bless you for this. I'm Bryce." He extended his hand.

"Well, it's nice to meet you Bryce." Sunshine took one hand off the wheel and shook his hand. "I'm Sunshine."

"The pleasure is mine. But I have to ask, is Sunshine your real name and is that your cell ringing?"

"Yes, it is my real name and yes my phone is ringing. It is my friend who specifically told me not to pick you up. So if you don't mind it's going to continue to ring."

"Wow! Your smile is amazing and your personality is so vibrant, so bright… just like your name."

"Ha ha, you've got jokes." Sunshine rolled her eyes.

"Look Bryce, don't make me throw you out." They both laughed. "Seriously, where are you going anyway?"

"I adore you." Bryce stared at Sunshine intrigued.

"Well, I don't know where that is. Hello? I'm kind of in a hurry and you are starting to freak me out."

"I apologize. I honestly meant no harm. It's 7700…"

"Not to cut you off or anything. But could you just enter it into my GPS. I am really pressed for time."

"Sure." Bryce leaned over to input the address but soon realized it had already been entered.

"You entered it that fast?" Sunshine inquired? "No, please don't be alarmed when I tell you we are going to the same place." Sunshine slammed on the brakes.

"Get out!"

"No, wait, I promise I work there. Look." Bryce smirked as he flashed his driver's license and studio pass. Sunshine looked both elated and confused.

"So you are one of the judges for my audition? That means you also work for Tre Paris?" He held up his index finger, placed it gently over Sunshine's lips to silence her.

"Yes and yes." Bryce pulled out his cell, called the studio. "Hey it's Bryce. I am still on my way but end the audition. I have what we've been searching for. Trust me she was born for this. Congratulations Sunshine, you have the part!"

Really God, just like that? Lord, I thank You!

Joy Marino is host of Matters of the Heart with Joy Marino, which airs every Tuesday night at 9:00 p.m. EST on The Survival Radio Christian Network. Tune in live at www.survivalradiochristiannetwork.com or call 347-237-4648.

Master Can You Use Me?

BY LARRY MCKENZIE

I once a heard somebody say, "Fortunate is the person who sees a need, recognizes the responsibility and actively becomes the answer."

Fresh out of college and still a very young age of 21 years old, a good friend of my mine introduced me to the Big Brothers and asked me to become a Big Brother.

Starting a new sales job, I had one thing on my mind and that was making money, and lots of it.

I grew up in a household with parents who were teachers and spent watching them spend time trying to impact the lives of their students, so I knew I wasn't interested in hanging out with some little kid; it was my time to do my thing. After all, I really questioned how much impact a 21-year-old could have, anyway.

Well, my friend finally convinced me that I would make a

good mentor and I became a Big Brother.

I was matched with a 13-year-old from a single-parent household who thought he was in charge of everything.

Jules and I both had a genuine love for the game of basketball, so when his middle-school team didn't have a coach, he volunteered his Big Brother. My response was, "You did what? You must be out of your mind, you didn't even ask me." Needless to say, he won the debate.

I became a Big Brother expecting to change a life of a young man and, instead, my life was forever changed.

It is because of my little brother that I found a love for coaching and would go on to coach youth basketball and later, a high school coach at a school in North Minneapolis. I thought I would be just be a basketball coach, but the job required a lot more.

Minneapolis Patrick Henry is located in one of the poorest neighborhoods in Minneapolis, MN. African-American males have a 28 percent graduation rate and a greater chance of going to prison than college.

Ninety-five percent of the students enrolled qualified for free and reduced lunch. Many of the families lived in poverty.

What is poverty? It is choosing between paying your rent or your electricity, and buying food or a bus card.

And even with working a job, often times the paycheck wasn't enough!

It wasn't enough to stop one of my star players from eating

Skittles for breakfast, or stealing food from the cafeteria for lunch.

It wasn't enough to stop a kid from sleeping on a different teammate's couch every night because he was homeless.

It didn't stop one of my players and his family from moving six times during the course of a just one school year.

Or 90 percent of all my players from using the community clinic for sports physical because they didn't have health insurance.

Because of the Village embracing what I was trying to do with kids, my kids and their families received a hand up instead of a handout.

I am proud to tell you that not only would these kids go on to win four consecutive state 3A titles, something that has only been accomplished twice in the 101-year history of Minnesota state basketball, they all enrolled in either a two-year or four-year college and ten now have college degrees.

Well, 30 years ago, I saw a need and I chose to give!

I recognized the responsibility and I became an advocate for a 13-year-old young man.

I volunteered as a Big Brother expecting to change a life and my life changed!

So I am asking you to join my team today and get off the sidelines and get into the game. If you have not given your time, talent or resources, I ask that you consider such and know that that any amount given can help change a life.

I thought I was too young to make a difference, but I did!

I thought I didn't have enough time to make a difference - remember, I was starting a new job - but I did!

I thought I didn't have enough money to make a difference, but I did!

Jules passed July 2013 at the young age of 46 years old, and I am forever grateful for the difference he made on my life.

And I am now as that championship coach, not just on the hardwood but in the game of life! I simply say "Jules, thank you!"

Because I allowed God to use me, I have been blessed to impact the lives of thousands of youth.

Why are you holding back? I ask today that you allow God to expand your territory. God is no respecter of person, if he did it for me, He will do it for you.

Larry McKenzie is host of Sports & Real Talk with Coach McKenzie, which airs every Sunday night at 7:30 p.m. EST on The Survival Radio Christian. Tune in live at www.survivalradiochristiannetwork.com or call 347-237-4648.

Smell the Rose

BY SHARON D. GREEN

"I am the rose of Sharon..." (Songs of Solomon 2:1a)

Let me testify of the goodness of God. Let me testify of His saving grace. Let me testify of a Father's Love, a brother's blood, and a Spirit's leading. Sounds good, as this is clearly the church's testimony. The best part of my testimony is that it's ALL TRUE. God the Father's Love is constant, consistently towards His children, and never changes (Malachi 3:6, Hebrews 13:8). The Blood of Jesus was shed over 2000 years ago to reconcile Christians back to the Father, so that we may live life in abundance. The Spirit of God is an awesome gift which helps, comforts, teaches, and is always available to lead. So what's the problem, why are overcoming, victorious, more than conquerors having a problem conquering, subduing, dominating, and being always triumphant (1 Corinthians 2:14) over a land that was created for our enjoyment (Psalm

115:16)?

SHERRY'S TETIMONY

Let's talk about it...Let's testify and learn one or two things from my testimony, in order to discover whose (Jesus', Mine, or Yours) testimony is worth publishing. My name is Sharon D. Green, fondly known as Sherry by friends and family. I am a native of Buffalo, New York, where I grew up in the St. John Baptist Church, attended a City Honors School, played a lot of basketball/sports in general, and did any and everything that I was bad enough to do. I was an athlete and a natural born leader, hence being able to change my name to Sherry, as Sharon was too boring. Therefore, being smart, competitive and, yes, cute, and confident (not conceited) opened up many doors to not only lead me in a way that I chose to go, but in a way that I've led a few folks with me.

I was well acquainted with church, I knew Jesus, but had no relationship with Him. There was no discipleship according to the Word, but the world was doing what it does - instill fear, exalt the lie, and teach nothing about faith. Growing up athletic allowed me to see life from a win or lose perspective, making good and evil relatively easy to see, but not necessarily the means for making the right choices. Needless to say, I've sown a lot of seed that multiplied a harvest of regret. The first harvest came in the form of divorce(s) and having attempted grown folks stuff at the young ages of 21 and 24. Although a tragic life event, well it should be for a Christian, I would like to say that if I knew that Malachi 2:16 was in the Bible, I would not have mastered the world's double anointing of broken covenant. I choose to believe that I am smart enough to have chosen 'growth' versus 'escape.' A choice that remains available to everyone reading this book.

> *"For the Lord God of Israel says that He hates divorce, for it covers one's garment with violence," Says the Lord of hosts. "Therefore, take heed to your spirit, that you do not deal treacherously."*

How does such an attack come to someone as loving, confident, and as smart as I am? The Blame Game was available back then, and remains alive and well today, but from someone who was created by God to tell the truth, it was never my crutch. It was only when I heard Joyce Meyer one day on TV that I received revelation of these life events. While watching Joyce on her show, "Enjoying Everyday Living," I heard her say, "When someone does something wrong to you, are they 'sowing' or are you 'reaping?'" For those of you who do not understand what this means, Genesis 8:22 tells us that "While the earth remains, there will be Seedtime and Harvest;" There is a harvest on every action taken. Well, after about two minutes of thought, I just started laughing, and thanking God that I never played the Blame Game with either of my husbands, who, by the way, grew up wonderfully, as I remembered and repented for the seeds sown throughout my young adult years. (LOL)

I'm sure that you're thinking, "If all Sharon had to go through was two divorces, that's no big deal in 2013," well, it gets better. It gets better because every time I finally choose to be led by He, Him, Holy Spirit, and live out the life Jesus died for me to have, it ALWAYS results in triumph (2 Corinthians 2:14), while the Enemy gets his tail WHOOPED!!! So, before I add on, know that I am fully persuaded that attacks of the enemy are a result of letting the hedge down (Ecclesiastes 10:8), and are a result of life as a FOOL (Proverbs 1:7), IGNORANT (Hosea 4:6), or just STUPID (Proverbs 12:1). I was a FOOL who despised wisdom and instruction; IGNORANT because YOU (LOL) had not grown up to teach me the right way to go. Check out the details of Hosea 4:6, which says "MY people are destroyed for a lack of knowledge, because YOU rejected..." It was not that the people did not know, Hosea 4:6 is talking about why they had no knowledge; the Priests failed to teach them. What a great excuse, and somewhat true, but the reality is that my attention to the world made it my schoolmaster. I was STUPID because I also hated correction. All of this brilliance made me vulnerable to spiritual attacks unaware.

IT GETS BETTER

While serving as a U.S. Army officer, leading Service Members and civilians in many different environments and circumstances, it was a personal honor to always set the example of Servant Leadership for my people. My people did not always appreciate servant leadership, because it affords the Leader the opportunity to remain fully engaged, and eliminates all of the excuses for poor job performance and customer service. At the end of the day, they loved me because servant leadership destroys the barriers of inferiority and promotes unity. I did not expect anything or request anything out of those who worked for me that I was not willing to do myself. My leadership style paid great dividends over the years, and elevated me to the Pinnacle level of leadership, where others do for you out of love, and not out of obligation. At the same time, I even maintained a successful basketball career, playing for the Army and an overseas German team, earning numerous awards, and this was after getting kicked off of my college basketball team...all because my mouth sowed one too many seeds. Amongst so much success and great relationships, it happened. I came under attack in my marriage and body all at the same time. The attacks came back-to-back resulting in five miscarriages, the live birth of twin boys, Johnell and Jannai, and death of my twin boys, one day after each other. Oh, and did I mention that adultery was a major player during this time too...and NO, I was not the one sowing the seeds... this time. However, I was truly reaping the harvest, which by the way, is always a multiplication of the seed sown.

HE ALWAYS LEADS US IN TRIUMPH

How did I handle so much loss and still lead my soldiers and civilians who did not miss a beat? It started off with a lot of disappointment, tears, and sleep, but by the third miscarriage, I was wide-awake, disappointed, and angry. The one thing that I knew without a doubt was that this should not be happening to me!!! I was using a biblical principle unaware, mourning for only 24 hours…Yes, I gave myself a time limit, and it worked! Isaiah 53:4, tells us that Jesus "Borne or grief and carried our sorrows;" and for that, I am sooooo thankful, so I let 'EM (Jesus) have it. Biblically unaware, I was convinced that I had no control over what was happening, and I refused to lie around and feel sorry for myself. I just knew that I was not supposed to be some pitiful, can't have a baby, feeling sorry for myself type person.

The night before I was rushed to the hospital because my cervix was opening, I stayed up, walking, washing and folding clothes, uncomfortable, and patiently waiting for my AM doctor's appointment. I chose not to bother my Drill Sergeant husband by waking him up to take me to the hospital. *Guess I probably should have chosen another time to be considerate of others.* The next day, I went to that appointment, where everyone in the hospital was in a complete panic...except for me. Panicking is not a leadership quality that I possess, primarily because it doesn't change the circumstances, and causes those around you to panic in excess. After arriving to the Medical College of Georgia, I checked in like as into a hotel, and remained in my nice private room, with a couch, for the next 22 days. Keep in mind that I was the Defense Military Pay Officer who was responsible for the Finance office that serviced active duty and reserve pay for an entire installation, Fort Gordon, Georgia. Clearly, my circumstances impacted more than just my family, as I was well known on the entire installation, having served in other capacities besides financial management.

On October 27, 1998, I gave birth to twin boys, at 24 weeks of pregnancy (Not Good), weighing 1lb, 7oz. and 1lb, 5oz. They were so small. I had never seen babies that small before, and had no idea of the responsibility of a neo-natal intensive care nurse, which was my only sister, Lisa's, profession. This was a challenging time that, although still married, was spent alone. My husband did not like coming to the hospital, as the job of Drill Sergeant at a training installation demands long hours. The boys lived for almost a month and never left the hospital. I did take some time off of work, but soon returned back to normal, leading an office of soldiers and civilians, assuring others that we are well equipped to overcome loss.

After the boys, I encountered miscarriage number six,

along with all of the drama that comes with a deployment, separation and second divorce. On August 7, 2003, I finally had a 6lbs, 2oz baby boy. So how did that happen without a husband? Don't judge (LOL), it did! I am now a U.S. Army Retired Service Disabled Veteran, proud mother of a kingdom obedient, disciple making, scholar athlete, virgin son named, John'al. My mom's name is Johnnie, and his dad and my dad are both referred to as Al. I named my son unaware that John means "Graced by Yahweh (God)." Wow...my grandmother's prayers were being answered, in spite of me.

Now that I have a male species child as a single parent, I can say with all certainty that he is definitely my greatest leadership challenge. John'al is my 'Sign of Completion', representing the 7th pregnancy, 'New Beginning,' representing the 8th child, and as previously stated, born in the 8th month, on the 7th day, at 33 weeks, which is 7 weeks too early. Not one thing was wrong with that boy. My body was the one having challenges from the blood thinners taken while pregnant. Today, I am confident of two TRUTHS, you don't have to have this testimony, and had I been biblically aware, equipped with faith and the right weapon (Word of God), I would not have this testimony either. As new creations are "Created in Christ Jesus," a place of refuge, a place where we die to self and become alive in Christ, it makes everything else a piece of cake.

Being an example for my son is priceless. Knowing the

unconditional love of a child forces you to make choices: choose to spiritually mature, or transfer generational curses. Well, I chose to mature and did what I do best: LEARN. Parenting is still a work in progress, but being able to deploy and enforce discipline via Skype was too cool. Since children love unconditionally, you have to teach them not to love, or trust, and to hate; while correction truly reciprocates love. Although, I often heed the advice received from a parenting book by Myles Monroe, where he reminded me of how "my hands were made for love." I can now report that living a life of obedience, as a student of the word of God, and example of servant leadership for my young son, comes with a peace that life apart from Holy Spirit will NEVER produce.

ROSES TESTIFY BEAUTY

Roses, like all flowers, are a product of seeds that died, took root, were watered, and then eventually grew. What makes the rose unique is that it depicts perfection and God's love for His sons (daughters). Perfection is only found in the truth, and it is the TRUTH that makes us FREE to live life to the fullest. My life, so far, is a reflection of just that. A life that died, received a Savior, took root in the Word, was watered through discipleship, and eventually, grew to fulfill the God-given assignment predestined by Father God before the beginning of time. *(For we are His workmanship, created in*

Christ Jesus for good works, which God prepared beforehand that we should walk in them [Ephesians 2:10]).

I was born on February 27th, the day that Noah and his family exited the boat on dry ground, and is the exact biblical number (G0227) for the Greek word Alethes; which means, true, speaking the truth, loving the truth, authentic, depicting nothing missing. No wonder I was blessed with the gift of being honest, regardless of person, place, or thing. However, it was only after being discipled by an Army Chaplain's Assistant named, MSG(R)/Dr. George Johnson Jr., while serving in Seoul, S. Korea, that I grew to appreciate God's love, my God-given name, Sharon, and the will of God for my protection, peace, and long life. Besides forming a leadership consulting firm, named to represent Truth, Alethes Consulting Group, LLC, I've added another weapon to my arsenal, another biblical truth of faith that I live by concerning evil attacks to Believers: "THE TESTIMONY OF JESUS IS THE SPIRIT OF PROPHECY" (Revelation 19:10). This truth now makes my testimony only valid, when it testifies to you that you DO NOT have to have my testimony…"BECAUSE THE BLOOD…"

LET ME TESTIFY THE TRUTH…THE REST OF THE STORY

In today's society, there is a resounding cry of "You Don't Know My Story." There is urgency for the world to know WHY you are you, or is it to reveal WHY you act and think like you do. However, in a book entitled, "Let Me Testify," I'm confident that I'm probably the only Christian Host that is bold enough to ask, WHY does the world need to know our story? Yes, I said it. WHY? We live in a dispensation of time that is under grace, where work cannot manifest the glory of God in our lives (Romans 11:6). The testimony of Jesus is our testimony, or it should be. In most cases, "Your Story" includes a testimony of overcoming some challenge of the past. This is going to hurt, but this is what I do...assist Christians to build a foundation of TRUTH, so that FAITH may always remain standing strong in your heart. The Bible is clear in Revelation 19:10b, **"Worship God! For the testimonyofJesus is the spirit of prophecy."** Philippians 3:13b, advises us to *"forget those things which are behind and reaching forward to those things which are ahead..."* Both scriptures are a challenge to do, when you can't GET YOU OFF OF YOUR MIND, and/or stop talking about a past that has no authority over your future. It also makes no sense to live a life with and in Christ, yet outside of faith, being unpleasing to God (Hebrews 11:6/Romans 8:8).

Don't get me wrong, if your story can help someone else NOT have your testimony, then it's a good report. Testimonies are designed for you to live a higher level of life at the 'experience' of someone else. They are designed to get faith stirred up in the life of someone else, but not as a sponsor for failure. Everything else violates Grace and presents the following problems:

1. Keeps you on your mind
2. Keeps you focused on the past
3. Makes the blood of Jesus shed on the cross over 2000 years ago, of no effect
4. Puts you back under the law where works manifested the love of God, or not
5. Has a root of evil, when God did not want us to have any "knowledge" of evil
6. Gives others the impression that struggle is key to spiritual growth; i.e. God uses evil to teach us good
7. Although possibly a WAY of God, who leads us in triumph (2 Corinthians 2:14); this is not the WILL of God who only has good and perfect for his children (James 2:17)
8. Lastly, your evil overcoming testimony is not the same Revelation 12:11 testimony (*And they overcame him by the blood of the Lamb and by the word of their testimony, and they did not love their lives to the death.*)

LET'S TESTIFY ABOUT REVELATION 12:11 – THE TRUE TESTIMONY

This particular Bible verse is often sited and rarely studied. It's often used as an excuse for Believers who struggle in life, as if it was the will of God to sacrifice His only begotten son, so that the family He so desperately wanted, could suffer too. NOT! The enemy has done a great job of painting this emotional picture of "it was the suffering that caused me to grow," in order to keep Christians out of faith and into the lie; a place of SELF. Self- centeredness was the same gift that allowed Satan to be slapped out of heaven, as depicted in Isaiah 14. Satan just could not get himself off of his mind.

> *"How you are fallen from heaven, O Lucifer, son of the morning! How you are cut down to the ground, You who weakened the nations! For you have said in your heart: 'I will ascend into heaven, I will exalt my throne above the stars of God; I will also sit on the mount of the congregation On the farthest sides of the north;I will ascend above the heights of the clouds,I will be like the Most High. Yet you shall be brought down to Sheol (Hell), to the lowest depths of the Pit".* (Isaiah 14:12-15)

The Christian misconception in the Body of Christ today is that the broke down, busted and disgusted testimony is responsible for overcoming the works of the devil. Yet, once again, please allow me to Testify about Revelation 12:11.

> *And they overcame him by the blood of the Lamb and by the word of their testimony, and they did not love their lives to the death. (Revelation 12:11)*

This scripture begins with the word "And," depicting a conjunction that connects the passage to the previous passage of scripture. In this occurrence, the word, "and," is connecting the word "they" to the previous passage. Who are THEY?"

> *Then I heard a loud voice saying in heaven, "Now salvation, and strength, and the kingdom of our God, and the power of His Christ have come, for the accuser of our brethren, who accused them before our God day and night, has been cast down. (Revelation 12:10)*

According to verse 10, THEY, is referring to Salvation, Strength, the Kingdom of our God, the Power of His Christ." Just from knowing who the 'they' represents, I personally do not see where a broke down, busted, and disgusted testimony could ever exist in conjunction to this passage...but let's not stop here.

"And they overcame" - To conquer, prevail

"Him" - Verse 10 tells us that "him" is the accuser of the brethren.

"by the blood of the Lamb" - The redeeming blood that was shed at Calvary by Jesus Christ. 1 Peter1:18-20, describes Jesus sacrifice on the cross like this:

"knowing that you were not redeemed with corruptible things, like silver or gold, from your aimless conduct received by tradition from your fathers, but with the precious blood of Christ, as of a lamb without blemish and without spot. He indeed was foreordained before the foundation of the world, but was manifest in these last times for YOU." (1 Peter 1:18-20)

"and by" - Conjunction. Salvation gives us a testimony found in the strength of God, gift of Holy Spirit, the kingdom of God that resides in us according to Luke 17:20-21, the power of God [Jesus Christ (1 Corinthians 1:24), Gospel of Christ (Romans 1:16), Right hand of God (Luke 22:69), Message of the Cross (1 Corinthians 1:18)]

"the word" - a word (as embodying an idea), a statement, a speech

"of their" - Who is talking? Verse 10 told us that "Their" is those who have received Jesus as their Lord and Savior, according to Roman 10:9. *"that if you confess with your mouth the Lord Jesus and believe in your heart that God has raised Him from the dead, you will be saved."*

"Testimony" - evidence given; evidence given of their salvation; good works on this side of the BLOOD

"and they did not love" - Conjunction of THEY to loving or being content

"their lives" - THEY chose to exchange their life for life in Christ "to the death" - physical or spiritual death; (figuratively) separation from the life (salvation) of God forever by dying without first experiencing death to self to receive His gift of salvation. SO...you still think that it's your testimony of struggle is attached to the will of God...? We all have them, what I call raggedy testimonies, but when you embrace the blood shed by Jesus in love, it makes it easy to keep Jesus on your mind, and in your heart as you "set your mind on things above, not on things on the earth." (Colossians 3:2) Verse 3 further states "For you died, and your life is hidden with Christ in God." Study of the Word has even changed my expectation for "Good and Perfect" (James 1:17) making everything else noticeable, out of order, and an insult to the blood of Jesus.

The Truth: The Christian testimony should be from a place of victory, and not from a place of defeat to victory. Although there are clearly challenges that come with being in this world, we must remember that the victory in Jesus made us complete at salvation; everything afterwards is either a by-product of obedience or disobedience. Ephesians 2:8-9 makes it clear that "For by grace you have been saved through faith, and that not of yourselves; it is the gift of God, not of works, lest anyone should boast." Yet the enemy has done another wonderful job of convincing Christians that we have to work to live in our Salvation. Believing the Word is starting to look like the exception. Most of you have heard and sung songs with words that say "He never said that it would be easy." Well, that's a lie, because He said that His yoke is easy and His burdens are light. *"Come to Me, all you who labor and are heavy laden, and I will give you rest. ²⁹ Take My yoke upon you and learn from Me, for I am gentle and lowly in heart, and you will find rest for your souls. (Matthews 22:28-29)"* As long as we, Christians, try to work in order to obtain/receive good, the Bible says in Romans 2:14, that we are a law to ourselves.

One of the most untaught truths is that there are three categories of people in the earth today: 1) Those who will reject Jesus as their Lord and Savior. 2) Those who received Jesus as Lord and Savior; however, due to being untaught or unchurched or disobedient, they never closed the gap between hearing, believing, receiving and living the word of God in faith while on the earth. 3) Those who have received Jesus as Lord and Savior, were led by Holy Spirit, chose to live by Faith, BELIEVED the Word, DID the Word, walked in the fear (reverence) of the Lord, and did not love their life to death. The works of these Believers will not burn up in the fire (1 Corinthians 3:13-15). They have crowns awaiting them in Paradise. Crowns that will be presented back to God in worship, depicting a life that was lived as unto the Lord. This is one of many untaught Truths in Christendom...a primary reason I decided to host a Christian Radio show, The Rose of Sharon Show.

The Rose of Sharon Show is rooted in Ephesians 4:15: *but,*

speaking the truth in love, may grow up in all things into Him who is the head—Christ— Since we are Believers who Believe, are representatives of Jesus and Sons of the most high God, each week listeners enjoy pinpoint interaction designed to not only grow up in all things, but to gain a better understanding that *"Love has been **PERFECTED** among us in this: that we may have boldness in the day of judgment; because as He is, so are we in this world."* This not a Christian entertainment show, but a weekly reminder of being "bought with a price," having a purpose to fulfill, as those who love God and keep His commands. Listeners have a choice to hear, believe, receive, and do, or not. My prayer is always that understanding takes place, listeners participate, and enjoy spiritual increase in the process. Smell the roses, the sweet aroma of the truth, and expect to grow in wisdom and favor, be empowered and made free by the truth, in order to depart ways, as a Proverbs 1:7 Fool, Proverbs 12:1 Stupid, but you'll never depart Hosea 4:6 Ignorant, because no one taught you in the way that you should go.

So let's do this...together...on one accord...led by the spirit of God, while *"looking unto Jesus, the author and finisher of our FAITH, who for the joy that was set before Him endured the cross, despising the shame, and has sat down at the right hand of the throne of God."* (Hebrews 12:2)

THERE IS A TESTIMONY OF LOVE WITH OUR NAME ON IT

Because of the Blood of Jesus...being led by Holy Spirit, I was able to...
1. Lay hands on the sick and they recovered
2. Lead thousands to Christ at one meeting
3. Raised the dead; opened blinded eyes and death ears
4. Enjoy whole family salvation for generations to come
5. Raised virgin children who are doing the same
6. Donate millions of dollars to the Kingdom monthly
7. Donate millions of dollars to people in need monthly
8. Provide Christian training responsible for Faith-filled Believers, believing, receiving, and doing

Now it's your turn...add to the list and "prove what is that Good, Acceptable and Perfect will of God." (Romans 12:2) TESTIFY ABOUT THAT!!!

"Oh, how I love Your law! It is my meditation all the day.

You, through Your commandments, make me wiser than my enemies; for they are ever with me.

*I have more understanding than all my teachers, for **Your testimonies are my meditation**.*

(Psalm 119:97-99)

Sharon D. Green is host of The Rose of Sharon Radio Show, which airs every Sunday night at 9:00 p.m. EST on The Survival Radio Christian. Tune in live at www.survivalradiochristiannetwork.com or call 347-237-4648.

Delivered for His Use

BY TANYA LEWIS

Life has many distractions that can steer you away from God and directly into the hands of the enemy. The sin that I had in my life separated me from God.

In my life, I allowed Satan to tempt me and seduce me through the lust of the flesh, eyes, and mind. As the old saying goes, "Everything that looks good isn't good for you." The deceiver sent his arsenal of sexual deviants and immorality to capture my soul as his prisoner. I found what I thought was happiness in women, drugs, and alcohol.

I have allowed God's love to free me and restore me from bondage. Don't allow your past or present circumstance to haunt you.

I am Tanya Lewis, nine years old. I am living in a single family home with my brother and my mother. I don't know where my father is right now but I heard that he is far from here. My mom is doing everything she can to raise my brother and me but she often gets sick and my brother and I go off to live in foster homes. I am not sure why I am in in these unfamiliar places but I want a normal life.

In these homes I was exposed to pastors' wives being unfaithful to their mates, girls bathing in the same tub and men who liked other men. My mind is young so therefore I can only adapt to what I see.

Age 12, my first experience sexually was with a school classmate. She invited me over and what I thought was an innocent touch turned into so much more. I didn't feel it was wrong because I was exposed to this and surely this couldn't be wrong.

Age 13, my father pops up and my brother and I are to go and stay with my dad because my mom is too sick to care for us. I was exposed to a new household once again. Things there were completely different. I didn't want to live with him. I stayed to myself but often looked for love in other people. While staying here I discovered my mom met someone and got married. I was never informed. Living with my father didn't last long and almost a year later my brother and I were reunited with my mother and her new husband.

My mom's husband was very strict and had a lot of rules. I did not like how I was treated. One evening after school I went over to a friend's house and because I missed curfew my clothes were placed outside on the curb. Sixteen years old and I was ready to hit the road again. I decided to move back with my father and his wife.

I am now entering in high school. No one ever took on the role of boyfriend with me. I wasn't exactly the most popular child. I was always in and out of places so I never had the opportunity to have anyone take on the role of boyfriend. I am once again in a new place and I don't take to anyone because I am not sure if I am going to move again. So I stay low key.

I hook up with these girls in high school and they begin to introduce me to the night life. We begin to hang out with guys but I am not interested in any part of that. There is one particular girl in the group who is checking me out and I notice her as well. I can tell that she is interested in me by her eye actions. I will not approach her. I feel myself attracted to her but not sure why I am having these feelings. I had never shared with anyone what happened in middle school. Is it wrong to feel the way I do? I am going to pretend that these feelings don't exist.

Things are going well. I am now 17, a senior in high school. I have a job and I love my life. I now have a group of friends and we party every weekend. I am finally stable or at least in my mind. I am in school and I am making my own money. What could possibly go wrong?

My father is preaching and my family is expected to go to church every Sunday, which is fine with me. He still had a lot of rules. My father was on his second marriage and things weren't peachy at home. Going out was my way to release the steam and frustration of things that were going on. One day my father and I got into a heated argument and I was asked to move out. I was 17 years old and I had no place to go but I had a job.

I began to stay at my girlfriend's house and other people's houses. Their parents began to question me and eventually I had to leave. This went on for a period of about 2 weeks.

I went to work and a co-worker who was trying to take me out for months now came and asked me if I was ok. I said yes I am fine. He asked me out once again and I decided to go. I had nowhere to go. What did I had to lose? We went out to a restaurant not far from our place of employment and one drank turned into two, two turned into three. I soon began to forget about every problem that I was having. He then asked if he could take me home. I told him I had no home and he insisted on getting me a room. I walk into a dark room and before I get all the way in, I was hit in the head and knocked backwards onto the bed. I felt hands around my neck and I passed out. I could still feel someone undressing me. I remember little but the next morning I woke up naked and in a bed full of blood. I was in the room alone. I showered, grabbed my things, and left.

I decided that it was time for me to go back home and try

to make things work out with my dad. The door was unlocked and I went in the house. I went into my old room and started to get clothes together. I head two voices come into the house. One was my dad's voice but the other was a woman whose voice I didn't recognize. I heard her ask whose kids are those in the pic. I heard his response, "Oh, I don't have kids." A tear fell down my face. I heard them in the bedroom doing adult things. I sat there, quietly, trying to wait for my time to leave out without being noticed. I overheard them taking a shower and that was my opportunity to run. I ran as fast as could. I heard the woman yell that she heard somebody.

Alone, hurt, and ashamed, I went to my father's car and cried. I slept in the car that night. I woke up early before he went to work, grabbed my things, and walked to the streets again. Where was I going to go now? What do I do? Not only was I hurt by my father but I had something valuable taken away from me.

I ran into the lady who had been checking me out and she asked me if I was ok. I didn't want to go into details with her but she invited me over to her house. We sat and she shared her life with me. I shared mine. She offered me a room to rent. I was relieved. I rented a room from her my senior year of high school and we got closer. As time went on we began an intimate relationship. Things were going well until secrets were being revealed. I didn't want to be a part of what was going on so I decided it was time to move on. It is almost time for me to graduate I had no plans whatsoever.

School is now out and I decide to move back with my mom and get a job. I had to get away from all of the mess that I was in and needed a new start. I started going to church with my mom and things were going well.

Months later, I met this guy who liked me from day one. He seemed to be nice but not really my type of guy. He asked me out and seemed to be the perfect escape to freedom. I agreed to go out with him and was shocked that I ended up having a good time. Months later, we started dating and began a family. There were rumors about a drug addiction but I wasn't going to judge his past.

A few years into the marriage, I discovered that these weren't just rumors. I discovered that he was in fact using crack cocaine and drinking heavily. I once again was hurt. I started hanging out and eventually I ran into the girl that I slept with in the eighth grade. We began to hang out more and more.

I was now with three kids and working and trying to have a normal life. Things at home weren't great. My husband and I had moved about six times in the past five years of our marriage and the money was short. I now get laid off of my job. Months later I get a job an hour away but my family needs the money so I accepted the job.

I had no idea what I was getting myself into. My job

commute was far but I had to do what I had to do. I began to notice that all of the women there were a little aggressive. I felt the same way that I felt in high school. I started to do my work and run out of the office immediately after. I wasn't sure what was going on but I had a family and wanted no parts of this life.

My home life is on the rocks with money issues and moving. Things got so bad we lived in a hotel for a while. This is not the life that I pictured for myself. Why is my life falling apart?

I get to work one day and people are sitting around and I make a comment and everyone laughs. One lady said, "T, you're funny. You have me cracking up!" I thanked her and they asked me to join them at lunch. I agreed to go and that started the friendship of a coworker and me. We would now start to have lunch and hang out after work every day. I now had a job that I enjoyed coming to.

My friend noticed that I started getting close and socializing with other coworkers. She said, "Tanya, don't mess with these women and leave your husband." I laughed. What were the chances of that happening?

Months pass and I get invited to this big after work event. My friend and I decided to go. There were so many women there who were gay. I was asked if I was family and I had no idea what that meant so said yes. Dinner went well and I ended up going to an after party with some of the ladies.

The music was loud and I kept seeing a lot of people go into this door, close it behind them and come out high or drunk or something. Some came out upbeat and ready to get the party started. I was feeling out of place. But when I was asked to dance, I declined. My coworker made me get up and dance. I started dancing by myself and before I knew it, other women were dancing around me. I thought to myself... 'What is going on?'

Months pass and I am hanging out more and more. I am coming home later and later. My kids and husband begin to question me. My husband's secret habits pick up and I am start not to care because I found my outlet of release.

One Friday, I came home and I noticed beer bottles outside on the porch. I walk in and my husband grabs me and pulls my hair. He then breaks my cell phone. I run to the store to calm down and he has me arrested.

I call a friend and stay with her a while and in three days when I can see my kids again I decided I am moving out. I then get my kids and move to Northern Virginia.

I am now completely out of the closet and move in with a lesbian friend whom I end up dating. I date her for three years and continue to live a homosexual lifestyle for six years. By now I am addicted to marijuana that my first girlfriend introduced me to and I'm partying on the regular.

Six years into the lifestyle, I get invited to church and I am delivered instantly. I am into my word and I am free.

Great things are happening to me.

God had me to share my story with women who deal with homosexuality who feel hurt and who don't know who they are in Christ.

I am now a full-time comedienne and an author of the book, Restoration. I stayed in the word of God and allowed his love to saturate me.

I have been delivered. That young lady who was all over the place is now serving God. Things happened bad in my life but I didn't allow my circumstances to hinder my future.

Tanya Lewis is host of Live & Laugh with Tanya and Michelle. Michelle Cousins co-hosts the show, which airs every Sunday night at 6:30 p.m. EST on The Survival Radio Christian Network. Tune in live at www.survivalradiochristiannetwork.com or call 347-237-4648.

Becoming Who I Was Born to Be

BY TERRELLE LEWIS

How is a young man able to properly define himself with a father whose mind is unstable, solely on the strength of a mother? I was raised by two God fearing parents, but their unstable marriage took its toll on me and my three siblings. When my mom and dad were separated and finally divorced, I wondered many years after, who God was, and if He truly existed. From a Child's point of view, how could God be so wonderful if he couldn't keep our family together? I never hated God, nor have I ever expressed any hatred toward the church, but as time went on, I became more and more confused.

At the age of sixteen, I was suffering from undiagnosed depression. Had it not been for my best friend's mother, who reintroduced me to Jesus Christ, I may have drifted into oblivion years ago. Her guidance and concern helped mold me for the greatest trials of my life and I thank God for sending her to me. The love and support that they showed me was priceless. I was in my tenth grade year of high school and living with my dad in Monroeville's Garden City. This suburban neighborhood had a profound effect on me from the time I was in kindergarten until I graduated high school.

I went to Wilkinsburg High School my ninth grade year and to tell you the truth, the experience was unforgettable. The black kids there were different from the ones from the suburbs. The black kids would clown you if you had lunch tickets at Monroeville. They would clown you if you couldn't afford to pay for your lunch with cash. They would clown you if you brought your lunch in a brown paper bag. I saw a social difference from suburb to borough or inner city black kids. Economically, in Wilkinsburg, everybody was poor so the jokes amongst us weren't solely based on "lack of money" issues. You got clowned based on your clothes or haircut. But more intensely, the inner city kids fought all the time. That was the thing I didn't miss. However, when I returned to go to Gateway school district I had a different perspective on self-identity. Being a young black man was complicated enough, but to be a "turn the other cheek" Christian on top of that was at that time an exercise of futility.

I began going to church and Bible study faithfully. I learned so much about the invisible, almighty God, Angels, demons, prophets and spirituality that I never stopped to consider why I was learning it. You see, I only believed in the idea of God. I never believed in God, because to believe in something is an action taken upon understanding what you're doing before you do it. I was reading and studying God's word, but I had no idea how real He was until I was consumed with only wanting to get to heaven and avoiding going to hell. Here is where my process began.

I loved God as a child. I feared God as a young man, but I feared going to hell more. This fear of hell started taking hold on me until I was consumed with guilt and fear. I was afraid to sin so I didn't have sex, I didn't drink or smoke, I didn't lie or steal or cheat to the best of my ability. I walked a straight and narrow path from my own perspective, but I wasn't serving the Lord. I became very introverted and built a wall so thick that my mind couldn't grasp what was real or what was illusion.

By the time I was 21 I was tormented with the thought of receiving the evidence of the Holy Spirit which I was told that when you speak in tongues that is when you finally have the Holy Spirit. I was lead to believe that after you accept Jesus Christ and believe that He was raised from the grave and ascended to the Father that I had to now tarry for the Holy Spirit. Tarry means to wait on, I thought it meant to go to church and beg and plead in front of the church, foam at the mouth, go into convulsions until the Holy Spirit finally gets inside you. Needless to say, I was wrong. But I went on with this belief and behavior for years until I finally started getting discouraged.

At twenty-one, I was on the phone with Mrs. Coleman one afternoon. I had reached the point of no return. I can't really remember our exact conversation, but she answered my redundant question that I kept repeatedly asking her. I was afraid to hang up the phone, but when I finally did, I left home with the idea that if I don't get to my church and get the Holy Spirit that night, I was going to die and go to hell. My heart and mind were filled with fear. My thoughts raced rapidly at every waiting moment.

I finally was on the last bus to catch that would have dropped me off right in front of my church, but I never got there. I sat in the front seat of the bus and had my face buried in my Bible trying to recite the verse of salvation. I began to rock back and forth rapidly and started feeling an overwhelming and powerful adrenaline pierce right through me until my actions caught the attention of the bus driver. He asked, "Are you ok buddy"? I interrupted my Biblical reciting with a short "yeah" and continued repeating the verse of salvation.

The church sat upon the middle of an inclined street and I was nearly there and for whatever reason having been convinced of its structural and spiritual safety, I knew that this was the only place on earth that I would find peace and God's Holy Spirit that day or I would otherwise die. I didn't realize that I had frightened several people on the bus acting the way I did and being 6'4" 225 lbs, black with a 7-inch afro, hanging cargo pants, boots and being quite muscular, that didn't help the situation either. The bus driver finally stopped the bus and took action, trying to get me off the bus. When he grabbed for my arm, I let out a cry of NO and scrambled for the back of the bus. I fell down and tried, with closed eyes, to find a tangible Holy Spirit.

Before I knew it, I was hearing voices and seeing flames and fire on everything. I then found myself fighting off several demons which turned out to be police officers. I was cuffed faced down with my hands and feet locked together and sustained a knee injury that I could barely feel at that moment. I was lifted off the bus floor and was carried backwards out into the cool summer breeze. I begged them not to take me to hell. I begged God to save me. I begged for my life at the top of my lungs like I had never screamed nor have ever since then again.

I was on an empty ambulance truck face down on the floor, still cuffed with my wrist and ankles locked together. I struggled so hard that my wrist began to bleed against the tightly locked handcuffs. The vehicle was going downhill and I was facing toward the back doors of the ambulance, believing that I was heading to hell. The inside of that ambulance was sweltering. If I could liken myself to Jesus when he sweated drops of blood while facing His destiny, I would have to say that at that moment I was, but I never opened my eyes long enough to see.

When the vehicle finally stopped and the doors suddenly swung open, a blast of cool air hit me. I was yanked up off the trucks floor and dropped onto a gurney. I had many hands upon me and I struggled to be free. The cuffs were removed and then replaced by the gurneys bars. I was rapidly pushed backwards once again and banged through sets of doors towards the ER. My ears were filled with the sounds of mocking laughter and scorning. When my gurney finally stopped I continued to shout back at the voices tormenting and mocking me.

My pants were ripped from my waist and the thought of being sodomized as my first sexual experience caused me to nearly sever my hands from the cuffs to protect my innocence. I then felt a sharp sting which gave no immediate peace, although the doctor pulling my pants back up gave me a bit of a reality check. I opened my eyes and stared at a Styrofoam cup being placed in front of me. I thought it to be vinegar, but as I tasted it cautiously, and I allowed the man holding the cup to tilt the cold water down my throat.

I started to feel the relief of the doctors and nurses and walks and floors. The voices receded and there were only about seven or eight people in the room that I was in, as opposed to eighty tormenting spirits ready to torture and torment me for all eternity. The man that gave me the water was a tall black man. His hair was salt and pepper grey and his face was stern and very concerned looking. He handed me another cup of water which I swallowed in about three gulps. The shot they gave me finally took its toll because when I finally shut my eyes I was awakened by the sound of crying.

My older brother sat on the bed I lay in and told me he was sorry for all the past misunderstandings that he and I had. My sheets were so white and the sun shined so brightly through the window that I thought I was in heaven laying on a cloud and that I was watching my brother from heaven's cloud. I felt a sudden sense of sorrow and I spoke as if I were a ghost in his ears saying, "Don't worry Eric, I'm still here."

I had several more experiences, nothing like the first one, but they all kept me returning in and out of mental institutions and hospitals. I struggled with my fears for years and was given the label of being Bi-Polar, schizo-effective, chemically imbalanced, mood disorders, etc. It wasn't until later that God revealed to me, what I thought was wrong with me, God called it right. Not once though did I speak against God or the Holy Spirit, for I remembered not to blaspheme the Holy Spirit.

Out of ignorance though, at times I blamed God for my mental state inwardly. I often thought God was so mad at me or had to punish me for not receiving His Holy Spirit. Then I received a message from another Christian's perspective and found out that the devil had been tormenting me with lies and deception. He was trying to abort my mission and my calling. I was also relieved to find out that God was loving me the whole time and was with me every trying, torturing step of the way. And my final revelation was that God is good all of the time and that He is in control and has purpose and blessings for me.

I must tell you, however, that my Bible studies did pay off. For all the years that I was studying and learning God's word, it was time to apply it to my life. When I started rejecting the sinful lifestyle that I was habitually doing, when I rejected the fear and believed what the Bible said about fear, God moved on me. When I spoke the word and
verses of the Bible which is God's word, God moved on me. "Faith comes from hearing," so when I continued and continue to speak and read and hear God's word, God continues to move in my life.

"Wisdom is the principle thing, therefore get wisdom, and with all thy getting, get understanding," I now believe in God, not just to believe if there is a God or the idea of a God. I believe in God because His word is powerful and potent and I continue to find out that the Holy Spirit began growing inside me the day I asked for it.

And as Jesus grows inside us we have to allow Him to spend time with His father by reading God's word. Jesus who lives in you now grows inside you when you read the Bible, fast and pray. So now what was labeled as a mental disorder,

I now have order and structure and purpose and a foundation in God to not fear or worry about anything. I'm not a "religious" person. I'm a man of God because I have a relationship, a connection with Him that grows daily as I search the scriptures, pray to my father in heaven and acknowledge Him in all my ways so that He can direct my path.

These days, I have established my career as a Professional Artist and Author. I am also Co-Host of Serene Motivations Radio and a Professional Security Officer. I've never called off of work and I've never been late. I spread the word of God every opportunity that I get. I am very pleased to be the man of God that I am today.

Terrelle Lewis is co-host along with Johnnette Young of Serene Motivations, which airs every Wednesday morning at 11:00 a.m. EST on The Survival Radio Christian Network. Tune in live at www.survivalradiochristiannetwork.com or call 347-237-4648.

Born Into Royalty

OFFSPRING OF THE GREAT KING

BY YOLANDA POWELL

But you are a chosen generation, a royal priesthood, a holy nation, His own special people, that you may proclaim the praises of Him who called you out of darkness into His marvelous light; who once were not a people but are now the people of God, who had not obtained mercy but now have obtained mercy. 1 Peter 2:9-10 (NKJV)

I am royalty! It's the most powerful reality of my thirty-three year reign with Jesus Christ. More than any other statement, I am royalty is my ultimate testimony. Being born into the family of God totally changed my life and altered my worldview. Before Christ, my self-evaluation, confused identity, and disturbed teen life left me bewildered and desperate for truth and light! I was stained by the effect of guilt and shame. But, Christ was the game-changer, and is forever my Healer and Hero. In every part of my being, He made the crooked areas straight, the rough patches smooth, and repositioned me for greatness beyond my wildest dreams.

Like a proverbial Cinderella, I went from rags to riches and was transformed from the inside out! He changed my garments and brought me into an enormous wardrobe of Kingship and Priesthood. If you are a born-again Believer in Jesus Christ, this is not just my story, but yours as well. Together, we are King's kids…the offspring of a Sovereign Lord, and joint-heirs with Christ.

By reading and meditating on I Peter 2:4-6; 9-10, we understand that we are a "chosen people," a "royal priesthood," and a "holy nation." What an esteemed position we have been given through Christ to represent and reflect God's nature and character before the entire world. We are also the "people of God," not a nation of subjects, but of sons and daughters. If God is a King, then we are also of the royal line. On Earth we govern and legislate on behalf of the Kingdom. How awesome is that!

THE JESUSHEIR CONCEPT

This is the premise of The Jesusheir Radio Show that I co-host weekly on the Survival Christian Radio Network with host Becky A. Davis. Becky received the "Jesusheir" brand from the Lord during a run one morning. Her vision and ministry platform is "to help Christians strengthen their discipleship skills, so that we can win more souls to Christ and build up the Kingdom of God." I love the term Jesusheir, because it is fresh and innovative and undergirds my mission as an apostolic leader, international speaker, and communications coach. So instead of telling people to "be saved,' with a scowl on our face, we can now ask them if they want to be a "Jesusheir" with a smile. This is a thrilling concept with regal ramifications and the ability to expand the Kingdom in enormous ways.

As Jesusheirs, we must learn how to operate as citizens of the Kingdom through both triumphant rulership, challenging situations and struggles. This comes from reading and studying the Word of God like a Manifesto - and nothing what our rights and privileges are as royal decision makers and regal authorities.

As Becky Davis writes, "Being a Jesusheir will help increase your discipleship skills to make you a better disciple to bring more souls to Christ. It's work that has great rewards." Without understanding the call to a royal family and a heritage of Grace, non-heirs (what we affectionately call unbelievers) have a lot of questions about they want to ask Jesusheirs (or Christians). Posted also on our website at www.jesusheir.com, here are the top 10 most frequently asked questions from non-heirs to Jesusheirs:

1. <u>What must I give up to become a Christian?</u> (view now)

2. Why is there evil and suffering in the world, if there is a God? (sign up to get video access)

3. I'm a good person, so why is that not good enough for Christians? (sign up to get video access)

4. How can a so called loving God send people to Hell?

5. <u>Why are there so many hypocrites in the church?</u> (view now)

6. Men wrote the bible, so why should I believe it?

7. You have to be perfect to be a Christian, and I'm not, so shouldn't I get myself together first?

8. Why do Christians act like they are perfect or better than everybody else?

9. How do you know there is a God?

10. Why should I go to church when my Christian friends do the same thing I do?

As you can see, we have a lot of work to do when it comes to reconciling non-heirs to the truth of the Gospel. They desperately need the "good news" that could lead to their conversion and rebirth. Most of all, they must know that being a child of God is an special honor, and that it comes with huge rewards and benefit to anyone who believes. John1:10 says, "He came to His own, and His own did not receive. But, as many as receive Him, to them He gave the right to become the children of God, to those who believe in His name who were born, not of blood, nor of the will of the flesh, nor of the will of man, but of God." This is a phenomenal invitation from above, and we must help non-heirs become Jesusheirs by sharing this incredible plan of redemption and restoration that flows out of the heart of a true and living God.

The Word of God further confirms this truth in Romans 8:17, "The Spirit Himself bears witness with our spirit that we are children of God, and if children, then heirs--heirs of God and joint heirs with Christ...." Being children of God is the essential message of the born-again experience. We are birthed in the Spirit by the Love of God, and take on the DNA of a loving and eternal Father. The plan of God was to RESTORE us back to Himself as dear children. His desire was to bring us into a FAMILY, and not a RELIGION.

THE CALL TO SONSHIP

"And because you are sons, God has sent forth the Spirit of His Son into your hearts, crying out Abba, Father!" Therefore, you are no longer a slave, but a son, and if a son, then an heir of God through Christ." Galatians 4:6-7

When I was growing up in church, the emphasis was always on our SIN and Shortcomings. Sermons were directed at getting us out of the "muck and mire" and loosed from the strongholds of darkness. Fiery preachers spit out hell fire and brimstone, attempting to scare us into the Heaven. It often had a reverse effect, and few of us every felt worthy to be called "the children of God." We were too dirty, unclean, and sinful...and no one would let you forget it! Little to no messages were placed on being translated in the Kingdom of God's dear Son or being a part of the sons of God (Romans 814). The text in verse 29 actually says that, "For whom He foreknew, He also predestined to be conformed to the image of His Son, the firstborn of many brethren." We are in the royal family with Christ! This is the will of God...not just to save us to regenerate us with divine destiny and purpose as HEIRS of His Kingdom and all that is His.

Jesus came to introduce mankind to the Father. More than anything, we needed to know that we have a Daddy, an Abba, a Papa that loves us unashamedly! As The Parable of the Lost Son reveals (Luke 15:11-32), the Father's heart is dedicated and committed to His children, even when we go astray or fall short. His open arms of compassion runs out to meet the rebellious son and to welcome him back with open arms. Then the love of the Father kills a fatted calf, throws a party and invites all the neighbors. If that wasn't enough, he then places shoes on his feet, a ring on his hand and a robe on his back. It is an extraordinary story of Paternal Love.

In the same way, Papa God openly declares that - through Christ - we are "in the family" with entitlements to all that our Father has. It is a relationship of heritage and inheritance.

BORN INTO ROYALTY

For me personally, this is the most exciting part of the New Covenant of Grace instituted through the shed blood of Jesus Christ. Not only do I have my sins forgiven and a "clean slate" with Papa God, but I am elevated to new heights of authority to "rule with Christ" in His eternal Kingdom. Together, we are involved in the manifold negotiations and operations of His vast domain and I am graciously responsible - through prayer, praise, prophesying and preaching to herald and advance the Kingdom. It is a partnership of divine proportions between Heaven and Earth and a Father and His children.

This realization that I am royalty is what led my husband, Pastor William, and I to begin Dominion International Ministries in late 2007. We wanted to establish a local church that ministered to Believers the "rule and reign" that belongs to them through Christ Jesus. So, our tagline is old and regal, "Dominion...An Embassy of Training and Development for Kings and Priests."

We are intentional not to create another "religious environment" where the people are subject to rules and tenants that are not life-giving and development. If Heaven is to be on Earth, and that is the Lord's Prayer...then we have to colonize this planet with the King's Sovereign Will to include His language, economy, educational system, worship order, social norms, cultural centers, and the like. In order to accomplish such an enormous task, the PEOPLE of God must have a mind-shift and a paradigm conversion. They must be trained and educated at a higher level, and introduced to such things as a culture of honor, kingdom protocol, etiquette, communications, social grace, the priestly office and its functions, spiritual engagement, kingly poise and posturing, musical refinement, artistic creativity, and much, much more.

At Dominion, we begin as early as pre-schoolers, whom we affectionately call, "TIMS", Toddlers In Ministry, to train and develop them as Kingdom citizens and Jesusheirs. It's not good enough to "wait until," because when it that going to be? The Kingdom is Now! We do the same things with the seniors and older one among us. Often times, they have to be "deprogrammed" from the religiosity of the traditional church; where everything was program centered, as opposed to people-centered and denominationally active, rather than Kingdom-infused. With them as well, we showcase the Fatherhood of God as a gift extended to us from Jesus Christ, and bring many of them in the reality of having a direct and personal relationship with "God our Father and the Lord Jesus Christ."

As Dr. Myles Monroe writes in his book, *Rediscovering the Kingdom*, "God is not interested in having subjects in His Kingdom. He wants only children, royal heirs to the treasures of His domain. Our mission as ambassadors of the Kingdom of

God is to bring those who are enslaved in the kingdom of darkness to Christ, the door, so that He can set them free to enter into their full citizenship in God's Kingdom of light."

Being born into royalty is an enormous privilege.

FROM RATCHET RAGS TO ROYAL ROBES

Sometimes, however, even when we have been through the "salvation experience" and have accepted Christ as Lord of our lives, we still walk around with a mentally that is foreign to our new positioning as Jesusheirs. We still need to change our garments and put on the items of royalty that come with the new birth.

This is where the Holy Spirit begins to array and activate us for His glory and honor. In ways that are not always easy to disclose, the Lord begins to strip from us the "ratchet rags" of regularity and commonness. He bathes us in the oil of gladness and cleans us from the filthy things that keep us among the base elements of life. He then redresses us in the Fine Fashions of Faith and places upon us His Royal Robes of Righteousness. This involves the elongated process of "renewing our mind."

The rags represent the old the robes the new. New clothing belongs to kings and priests and rags to the peasants and street folks. If Jesus is the King of kings and the Lord of lords, and we are "joint-heirs" with Him, then is clear that we are no longer "common" and never again should be referred to as "sinners and worms" - as we were once told. We are brand spanking new! We have been CHANGED, and that transformation must be celebrated with complete NEWNESS. Isn't that supported by Paul's words to the church at Corinth? "Therefore, if anyone is in Christ, he is a new creation; old things have passed away; behold all things have become new (5:19)."

HIS SIGNATURE DESIGN: READ THE LABEL

This spiritual wardrobe is filled with finery and the very best of God's royal designs. We are admonished by seasoned women like Urenna Crawford, a speaker, coach, and author of the book *LEGACY "The Things Mommy Said to Me, I Say Again to You,"* to "read the label." Urenna (or Mama C, as she is affectionately called) spoke powerfully on The Jesusheir Radio Show recently about our creative design and who we are in Christ Jesus. Her statement "Read the Label," seemed to jump off the page and bring clarity to the Kingdom message that we herald each week.

When someone wants to feel good about himself or impress a friend, he'll often purchase items that is made by a top designer. Wearing that expensive item and showcasing its quality and rarity makes him feel good about himself and seems to clarify his worth, identity, and dignity in a strange way. Well, that's what happens to us when we take on the value and importance of a Kingdom life. Our spiritual worth, personal identity, and overall dignity as a human being is lifted to impossible heights. Why? Because the righteous robes we acquire through conversion cost Jesus His very life! Blood was shed, and an act of sacrifice was endured on our behalf. This increases the VALUE of our lives, and makes us wealthy in ways we don't even know. That's why Mama C says, "Read the Label!"

DRAPED, DRESSED, AND DESTINED TO RULE

Through life-giving association with a King and the rebirth of my spirit through the Ancient of Days, I have entered the MIRACLE of translation…where I am adopted into the family of God. On that day, the angels rejoiced, the realms of glory went into a thunderous praise and the God-head smiled a sigh of relief and exaltation. Could it be that life is that significant to the Father? Could it be that like a Shepherd, He will leave the 99 and go after the 1? Could it be that He is so paternal that shares His eternal kingdom with me and you and is simply the joy of parenting and doting on His offspring? I have come to know that He counts my life as extremely valuable, that He sent His only begotten son to die and make me a (female) son through the new birth and that it is the Father's GOOD PLEASURE to GIVE me the Kingdom! Read and meditate on

Luke 12. Such stories told through the lens of Christ should be revisited over and over again.

Truly, I have been draped, dressed, and destined for greatness! Greatness is within my loins...God the Father put it there from Genesis chapter 1, when He said, "Let us make Man in our Image and after our Likeness..." After that, desire was marred by sin, disobedience, and rebellion. Jesus returned to that same Garden and redeemed Man back, restoring Him to the position of ruling and reigning with Christ...so that He could "have Dominion!"

So I am convinced that there has always been a king in me, as it is in you! Not only does the Sovereign Lord not make junk and have throwaway children, but He is producing and birthing kings and priests who will "handle His affairs" and "do His bidding," on the Earth. Knowing such things levels the playing field, and gives us Jesusheirs a set of keys and total access to the Kingdom. This is a game-changer indeed! So just Let Me Testify to the miraculous wonders of Kingdom life, the joys of royal citizenship, and the reality of being a Jesusheir!

Yolanda Powell is co-host of Jesusheir Radio with host Becky Davis. The show airs every Tuesday morning at 10 a.m. EST on The Survival Radio Christian Network. Tune in live at www.survivalradiochristiannetwork.com or call 347-237-4648.

www.ingramcontent.com/pod-product-compliance
Lightning Source LLC
Chambersburg PA
CBHW051806040426
42446CB00007B/545